D1738838

Literature, Judges and the Law

Literature, Judges and the Law

W.N. OSBOROUGH

FOUR COURTS PRESS

Set in 10.5 on 14 point Caslon
by Mark Heslington Ltd, Scarborough, North Yorkshire for
FOUR COURTS PRESS
7 Malpas Street, Dublin 8, Ireland
e-mail: info@fourcourtspress.ie
and in North America
FOUR COURTS PRESS
c/o ISBS, 920 N.E. 58th Avenue, Suite 300, Portland, OR 97213

A catalogue record for this title
is available from the British Library.

ISBN 978-1-84682-079-3

Printed in Great Britain
by Antony Rowe Ltd, Chippenham, Wilts.

Contents

Preface

The reasoned judgments penned by holders of judicial office constitute a genre of literature that has commanded little notice and even less interest outside the ranks of the legal profession and those who would aspire to join it. Novice lawyers – law students – are obliged for educational purposes to read, and to familiarize themselves with, a very large number of them, and should they eventually attach themselves to the profession, the recollection of the essence of a proportion of them, and the skill they ought to have acquired in the course of their training to locate and to interpret others not previously brought to their attention, should stand them in excellent stead.

It would have to be conceded that most judgments do not make palatable reading. From time to time, however, mercifully, it is different. You can, in thumbing through the law reports, chance on a topic or a judicial discussion that may either brighten the day or illuminate some portion of contemporary sociology or forgotten history. Problems in Celtic mythology,[1] spousal burial in a coffin designed to defeat the predation of resurrectionists,[2] extra-terrestrials and copyright law,[3] the management of foxhounds,[4] the throng at a railway station,[5] the speed of the Japanese advance into Burma in 1942:[6] enlightenment on just such an eclectic mix of themes is there to be had on any excursion to a well-stocked law library. And on so much else besides, since serendipity there reigns supreme.

But mastering the law – the declared object behind the insistence on reading and digesting such variegated material – does not come easily. Judgments of our practitioners can be of an unwholesome length. Seven judges of the Irish Supreme Court, handing down their judgments in *Maguire v. Ardagh*, contributed no less than 267 pages to a volume of the Irish Reports for 2002.[7]

1 *A-G v. Trustees of the British Museum* [1903] 2 Ch. 598. 2 *Gilbert v. Buzzard* (1821) 2 Hag. Con. 333, 161 ER 761. The resurrection-man's goods, Jerry Cruncher, senior tells Jerry Cruncher, junior, 'is a branch of Scientific goods': Charles Dickens, *A tale of two cities* (London, 1859), bk. 1, ch. 14. 3 *Cummings v. Bond* [1927] 1 Ch. 167. 4 *Barrett v. Irvine* [1907] 2 IR 462: see below, p. 4. 5 *Great Western Railway Co. v. Bunch* (1888) 13 App. Cas. 31 at 55 (speech of Lord Macnaghten). 6 *Burmah Oil Co. Ltd. v. Lord Advocate* [1965] AC 75. 7 [2002] 1 IR 385 at 475–742 (judgments of each of the seven judges sitting on the Supreme Court on the occasion). The judgment of the 3-man Divisional High Court in the case occupies 56 pages: [2002] 1 IR 391–447, and counsel's arguments before the Supreme Court another 27: [2002] 1 IR 447–74.

In England in 1977, the judgment of the vice-chancellor, Sir Robert Megarry, in *Tito v. Waddell (no.2)* occupied 241 pages in the Chancery reports for that year (and 216 pages in the Weekly Law Reports or 194 pages in the All England Law Reports in their respective versions).[8] A Scots judge, Lord Nimmo Smith, can now perhaps lay claim to a record – 594 pages for his judgment in *McTear v. Imperial Tobacco Ltd*, a judgment to be found in a separate volume of Session Cases for 2005.[9] Longwindedness, undoubtedly, can be viewed as a vice and a disincentive to learning,[10] but whether judges are to be deemed solely to blame admits of genuine differences of opinion. The subject-matter of the litigious controversy itself, the complex character of applicable legal doctrine, or the desideratum of a plurality of judgments in cases of significant legal or political impact can each one be urged in extenuation.

The thrust of the present volume is to examine one singular facet of judgments generated within the tradition of the Common Law: the use of literary quotation and allusion. The hope is expressed that lawyers and non-lawyers alike may find it of some value: the former through encountering judgments and judicial extracts of which they may previously have been unaware, the latter through learning something of how members of the judiciary have gone about their business of preparing judgments.

I am indebted to Valerie Rodgers for first identifying for me the passage from Hesiod which is featured in a rare case, but one of a mere handful, where quotations from classical Greek authors have tellingly been employed, and to my colleague, James Casey, for many additions to my original listings of Irish cases deserving of a mention. Six or so additional illustrations were suggested by Sir Robert Megarry's first published legal miscellany.[11] But it was the result of being required, in the course of an academic career straddling two continents and four different university law schools, to teach, and thus fully myself to attempt to understand, an unusual spread of branches of law that first introduced me to the vast majority of judgments surveyed here. These judgments, with their accompanying several quotations and allusions, all listed in the pages of the ensuing compendium, it is now my pleasure to present.

For secretarial assistance, I should like to thank Peggy Morgan, Natalia Zadorozhnyaya and my daughter Rachel Lewis.

8 [1977] Ch. 106–347, [1977] 2 WLR 489–712, [1977] 3 All ER 129–323. **9** 2005 2 SC 1–569 (or with an added table of cases and, remarkably, an index) – 594. **10** Cf. F.H. Newark, 'The anatomy of a law report', *NILQ*, xvi (1965), 371, reprinted in *Elegantia juris: selected writings of F. H. Newark*, ed. F.J. McIvor (Belfast, 1973), p.258. **11** R.E. Megarry, *Miscellany-at-law: a diversion for lawyers and others* (London, 1955).

INTRODUCTION

Of whales and foxes and other preliminary matters

The lawsuits over whales introduced to the reader in chapters 89 and 90 of Herman Melville's novel *Moby Dick*, though unannounced, ought not to be regarded as unexpected. Interspersed with Melville's saga of Captain Ahab of the *Pequod*'s fatal pursuit of the Great White Whale we are made the recipients of a very great deal of information and lore regarding whales: a veritable New Naturalist volume is being manufactured for the reader before his very eyes (and the enterprise continues after chapters 89 and 90).

Chapter 89 records 'a curious case of whale-trover litigated in England' in the early years of the nineteenth century. Counsel for the defendants, Melville tells us, was Thomas Erskine and the judge was the chief justice of king's bench, Lord Ellenborough (who joined the Ministry of All the Talents in 1806 and was the last chief justice to sit in the cabinet). Whale-trover cases feature in the English Reports for 1788 (*Littledale v. Scaith*)[1] and 1808 (*Fennings v. Lord Grenville*).[2] Melville's case is neither of these, but can be confidently dated even so to the period between April 1802, when Ellenborough succeeded Lord Kenyon as chief justice of King's Bench, and February 1806, when Erskine became lord chancellor. Melville's case of whale-trover was one, where, so the author goes on,

> the plaintiffs set forth that after a hard chase of a whale in the Northern seas; and when indeed they (the plaintiffs) had succeeded in harpooning the fish, they were at last, through peril of their lives, obliged to forsake not only their lines, but their boat itself.

The genesis of the eventual lawsuit is indicated by what happened next:

> Ultimately the defendants (the crew of another ship) came up with the whale, struck, killed, seized, and finally appropriated it before the very eyes of the plaintiffs. And when those defendants were remonstrated with, their captain snapped his fingers in the plaintiffs' teeth, and assured them that by way of doxology to the deed he had done, he would now retain their line, harpoons, and boat, which had remained attached to the whale at the time

1 1 Taunt. 243n, 127 ER 826n. 2 1 Taunt. 241, 127 ER 825.

> of the seizure. Wherefore the plaintiffs now sued for the recovery of the value of their whale, line, harpoons, and boat.

The outcome was, indeed, a judgment worthy of Solomon: Ellenborough decreed in favour of the plaintiffs in regard to their boat, but awarded the controverted whale, harpoons and line to the defendants. (Later United States authority, and, in particular, *Ghen v. Rich*, a decision of Judge Nelson, a federal district judge in Massachusetts in 1881,[3] reached a different conclusion, averring that the boat that first struck an iron into the whale was by local custom given possession of the whale and that the custom was reasonable and valid.)

Ownership of a whale that had been beached at Whitstable on the south coast of England in 1829 was at issue in the second lawsuit which Melville recounts. Here there is no difficulty in finding the case in the law reports. It is *Lord Warden and Admiral of the Cinque Ports v. His Majesty in his Office of Admiralty*, an 1831 decision of Dr Phillimore, the judge of the court of Admiralty.[4]

Melville indulges in a little journalistic licence when furnishing his recital of the facts. 'It seems', he relates,

> that some honest mariners of Dover, or Sandwich, or some one of the Cinque Ports, had after a hard chase succeeded in killing and beaching a fine whale which they had originally descried afar off from the shore.

The dénouement, however, was set to darken the expectations thereby aroused:

> Now when these poor sun-burnt mariners, bare-footed, and with their trousers rolled high up on their eely legs, had wearily hauled their fat fish high and dry, promising themselves a good £150 from the precious oil and bone; and in fantasy sipping rare tea with their wives, and good ale with their cronies, upon the strength of their respective shares; up steps a very learned and most Christian and charitable gentleman, with a copy of Blackstone under his arm; and laying it upon the whale's head, he says – 'Hand off! this fish, my masters, is a Fast-Fish. I seize it as the Lord Warden's.'

In fact, as the proceedings before Dr Phillimore make plain, there had been controversy over whether the whale belonged to the lord warden under some form of delegation from the crown or to the crown outright. The whale was a

3 8 Fed. 159. 4 2 Hagg. 438, 166 ER 304.

royal fish, and there was thus no question of Melville's 'sun-burnt mariners' having any claim at all. The lord warden at the time – and the successor to Lord Liverpool who had died in late 1828 – was the duke of Wellington, the victor at Waterloo in 1815 and for a short period (January 1828 – November 1830) prime minister. Dr Phillimore, in his judgment on the controversy, held that the lord warden had prior rights to the whale by virtue of a delegation from the crown, which, truly interpreted, established the duke of Wellington's claim.

Wellington, despite the remonstrances of a local clergyman, Melville infers, did nothing to reward the mariners – in the original, the masters and crews of seven oyster smacks – who had captured and beached the whale. 'Is this', the author sourly inquires, 'the still militant old man, standing at the corners of the three kingdoms, on all hands coercing alms of beggars?' In an exactly contemporary case, however, Wellington is depicted as having behaved rather more generously. Forty salvage men from Bexhill had in 1830 petitioned Wellington as lord warden in regard to a Dutch ship buried in the sand from which they had sought to extricate the cargo of timber and glass only to be told that the cargo belonged to the customs and the lord warden. Wellington responded by authorising the allowance to the men of £100's worth of cargo the first year, with the residue being shared equally with the customs thereafter, but not so as to prejudice the rights of any future lords warden.[5]

Moby Dick is a trifle unusual in that in chapters 89 and 90 the content is inspired by no less than two separate lawsuits. It is much more commonplace for the writer of fiction to have borrowed his ideas from a single instance of litigation. So it is with both Francis MacManus's *The greatest of these* (Dublin, 1943) and Thomas Kilroy's *The big chapel* (London, 1971), two Irish novels, loosely but very differently constructed around the dispute between the real-life Roman Catholic parish priest of Callan, Co. Kilkenny, the Revd Robert O'Keeffe, and his ecclesiastical superiors which climaxed in the extraordinary defamation case of *O'Keeffe v. Cardinal Cullen*. The case itself is reported at length in the Irish law reports, if only on a preliminary, but by no means insubstantial, legal point.[6] Kilroy's discussion in particular of the law on qualified privilege would seem to display a considerable indebtedness to the original.[7]

Similarly, other pieces of fiction have been driven by the author's reworking of some single *cause célèbre*. In *The Count of Monte Cristo* (1846), for example, Alexandre Dumas, père was to base his tale of Edmond Dantès on the case of

5 Elizabeth Longford, *Wellington: pillar of state* (London, 1972), pp 249–50. 6 (1873) IR 7 CL 319. 7 See further W. Nial Osborough, 'Another country, other days: revisiting Thomas Kilroy's *The big chapel*', *Irish University Review*, xxxii (2002), 39.

François Picaud who, wrongfully imprisoned under the Empire, returned after 1814 to exact violent retribution on his accusers.[8]

This book is not about creators of literature dipping into the law. It is rather about the reverse traffic, the writer of the judicial judgment dipping into literature.

Some further introductory remarks are in order.

First, not every species of court judgment lends itself to the incorporation of some literary allusion or, at least, has been so regarded. Take lawsuits touching on aspects of foxhunting, for instance. Of these there have been plenty. In New York state in 1805 the state Supreme Court had to pronounce on a claim brought by one Post against one Pierson who had shot a fox being hunted at the time by the former, a circumstance well known to Pierson. A majority held that Pierson's act 'was productive of no injury or damage for which a legal remedy can be applied': *Pierson v. Post*.[9] A vigorous dissent from Judge Livingston waxed eloquent: 'Who', he asked,

> would keep a pack of hounds; or what gentleman, at the sound of the horn and at peep of day would mount his steed, and for hours together sub jove frigido or a vertical sun, pursue the windings of this wily quadruped, if, just as night came on, and his stratagems and strength were nearly exhausted, a saucy intruder, who had not shared in the honors or labours of the chase, were permitted to come in at the death, and bear away in triumph the object of pursuit?

From this sort of language, one anticipated even more, but in fact, there is no literary allusion or quotation.

Nor is there in the well-known Irish case of *Barrett v. Irvine* (1907),[10] where the then Irish lord chief justice, Lord O'Brien of Kilfenora, furnished, in a gratuitous piece of purple prose, a description of a local pack of foxhounds – some compensation, therefore, for the all-too-obvious lacuna just adverted to. *Barrett v. Irvine* raised a point in the law of agency. Could, in the circumstances revealed, Marjory Irvine, the mother of Hugh Irvine, a minor but, despite his minority, the master of the Roscarberry Foxhounds in west Co. Cork, be made answerable for the purchase price of a horse, Easter Boy, that Hugh had bought from one Edward Barrett? At the Cork spring assizes in 1907 Mr Justice

8 Peter France (ed.), *The new Oxford companion to literature in French* (Oxford, 1995), pp 192–3.
9 3 Caines 175. **10** [1907] 2 IR 462.

Johnson had awarded Barrett £60 and his costs, but the King's Bench Division (Lord O'Brien, Mr Justice Gibson and Mr Justice Kenny) set aside that finding on the grounds that the evidence failed to prove any general agency in Hugh for which his mother could be made answerable, an adjudication unsuccessfully appealed to the Court of Appeal.[11]

Where the evidence was derived regarding the pack of hounds over which Hugh Irvine presided does not emerge, but nothing detracts from Lord O'Brien's description of the pack, which certainly has the ring of truth:[12]

> The Roscarberry pack was certainly interesting by reason of its diversified character. Variety has a charm of its own. What is unique is always attractive. The pack was composed of all sorts and conditions of hunting dogs – uniform neither in size nor pace nor breeding – and though it was styled the 'Roscarberry Foxhounds' it could boast of only one pure-bred foxhound – *lucus a non lucendo*. The proclivities of the pack were as diversified as its composition; it pursued with equal ardour every description of quadruped, whatever the nature of the scent. I am not sure that the feathered tribe was altogether without some measure of attention. However, though the ménage at Roscarberry was not quite up to Leicestershire standard, I feel quite certain that the heart of the young Master was, so far as related to physical courage, in the right place, and that he often afforded a good sport, and that the followers of the pack had not infrequently, to use an expression amongst hunting men, 'a clinking run'.

Popular agitation in recent days in Britain to proscribe foxhunting, agitation culminating in legislation passed both by the Scottish Parliament and at Westminster, has precipitated an amount of litigation where once more the focus of attention has been on foxhunting itself. But it remains the case that any temptation there may have been to append literary allusions – and of the latter there was no shortage – was to be stoutly resisted.

This sequence of lawsuits may be said to commence with *R. v. Somerset County Council, ex parte Fewings*,[13] technically a case concerned with deer-

11 [1907] 2 IR at 474. **12** [1907] 2 IR at 468–9. The extract is included in Frank O'Connor (ed.), *A book of Ireland* (London and Glasgow, 1959), pp 154–5. **13** [1995] 1 All ER 513. Cases where the focus was on efforts to reverse policies opposed to hunting with dogs constitute a subsidiary stratum: see *Scott v. National Trust for Places of Historic Interest or Natural Beauty* [1998] 2 All ER 705 (National Trust's prohibition on deerhunting with hounds at its lands on Exmoor, Devon and the Quantock Hills, Somerset), and *Royal Society for the Prevention of Cruelty to Animals v. A.G.* [2002] 1 WLR 448 (RSPCA's seeking of guidance on validity of plan to deny member-

hunting not foxhunting. Fewings and other individuals ran the Quantock Stag Hounds and had been accustomed to hunt deer with their hounds over local authority land at Ower Stowey Customs Common. In August 1993, however, Somerset County Council, by a vote of 26 to 22, decided to prohibit deer-hunting on their lands. Mr Justice Laws decided that the ban was ultra vires the county council and that decision was upheld by a majority of the Court of Appeal (Sir Thomas Bingham, master of the rolls, Lord Justice Swinton Thomas, Lord Justice Simon Brown dissenting), albeit on rather different grounds.[14] We will be returning to the language employed by the judges in the *Fewings* case.

The tempo of litigation quickened with the enactment by the Scottish parliament in 2002 of its Protection of Wild Mammals Act and by the Westminster parliament in 2004 of its Hunting Act. Both measures made the hunting of a wild mammal with a dog an offence.

The Scottish initiative has been before the Court of Session on a number of occasions. In *Whaley v. Lord Watson*, in 2000,[15] the master of the Berwickshire Hunt sought an order from the courts to interdict Lord Watson, a member of the Scottish parliament, from introducing his bill banning hunting. The somewhat tenuous basis of the application was that Lord Watson had received assistance from a pressure group, the Scottish Campaign against Hunting with Dogs, in the promoting and drafting of the projected measure. The application was refused by the lord ordinary, Lord Johnston, and that refusal was endorsed by the Inner House (Lord President Rodger, Lords Prosser and Morrison).[16]

Following enactment of the controversial Scots measure in 2002, two separate challenges were to be mounted, based largely on the contention that the Act contravened the European Convention on Human Rights, a contention, as it happens, that was to be shot down in a long article appearing in the *European Human Rights Law Review*.[17] Both sets of challenge were to fail. In *Adams v. Advocate General*, the lord ordinary, Lord Nimmo Smith, rejected arguments presented on behalf of Adams, who managed foxhounds for the Duke of Buccleuch's Hunt, and of other petitioners including an erstwhile Master of the Lauderdale Hunt,[18] and that adjudication was subsequently endorsed by the Inner House (Lord Justice-Clerk Gill, Lords MacFadyen and Abernethy) in a case somewhat differently entitled *Adams v. Scottish Ministers*.[19] The outcome was identical when Whaley returned to the fray, arguing that the Protection of

ship to individuals intent on securing reversal of its policy opposed to hunting with dogs). **14** [1995] 3 All ER 20. **15** 2000 SC 125. **16** 2000 SC 340. **17** Rabinder Singh and David Thomas, 'Human rights implications of a ban on hunting with dogs', *European Human Rights Law Review*, vii (2002), 28. **18** 2003 SC 171. **19** 2004 SC 665.

Wild Mammals (Scotland) Act contravened both the European Convention on Human Rights and certain international obligations of the United Kingdom. In another lengthy judgment the lord ordinary, Lord Brodie, rejected both contentions: *Whaley v. Lord Advocate.*[20]

The legal attack on the legislation passed at Westminster in 2004, the Hunting Act of that year, was rather more oblique. The measure had been opposed by the House of Lords and only came into effect through the use of the Parliament Acts of 1911 and 1949. The contention advanced on behalf of the Countryside Alliance, in seeking to strike down the Act itself, was that the Parliament Act of 1949 was itself invalid and of no effect since its passage had been secured without the assent of the House of Lords. Without totally dismissing the argument that the Parliament Act procedures could not be employed to effect major constitutional changes, the House of Lords, on appeal from the Court of Appeal (itself hearing an appeal from the Queen's Bench Division), held that the activation of the Parliament Act procedures to secure passage of the Hunting Act could not be constitutionally faulted and that the Parliament Act of 1949 was itself valid.[21]

In none of this more recent litigation, whether in England or Scotland, has any member of the judiciary incorporated literary allusions or literary quotations into their judgments. I suspect the temptation could well have been there. Oscar Wilde puts into the lips of Lord Illingworth in *A woman of no importance* (1893) the well-known observation:[22]

> The English country gentleman galloping after a fox – the unspeakable in full pursuit of the uneatable.

Rather more quotations are available to those who would support the other side of the argument. There is Trollope; there are (there is) Somerville and Ross; and there is Surtees, particularly speaking through his character Jorrocks, the fox-hunting grocer. In *Handley Cross* (1843), Jorrocks declaims: 'Tell me a man's a foxhunter, and I loves him at once'.[23] Rather earlier in the novel, there had been this encomium of the fox-hunt:[24]

> 'Unting is all that's worth living for – all time is lost wot is not spent in 'unting – it is like the hair we breathe – if we have it not we die – it's the sport of Kings, the image of war without its guilt, and only four-and-twenty per cent of its danger.

20 2004 SC 78. **21** *R. (Jackson) v. A.G.* [2006] 1 AC 262, affirming the Court of Appeal: [2005] QB 579, [2005] 2 WLR 866. **22** Act 1. **23** Ch. 11. **24** Ch. 7.

The reticence of the judiciary – remarkable in the case of the Scottish judges, when a comparison is drawn with the conduct of Lord Anderson in *Rothfield v. North British Ry. Co.*,[25] the 1920 case touching on the history of Scottish inns – is, I think, easy enough to understand. Where the subject-matter of the litigious dispute is politically contentious – as deerhunting and foxhunting have been, are and will continue to be – prudence dictates a course of conduct, mandating the soberest of reasoning in the judicial judgment. Intellectual pyrotechnics are not recommended, indeed are to be positively avoided, and if that has meant declining to employ an apt quotation from the days when the judges went hunting themselves, so be it.

In the case concerned with the ban that Somerset County Council placed on deerhunting, a case preoccupied with the scope of judicial review, Mr Justice Laws went out of his way to stress that he was only concerned with the legality of what the local authority had done, not with the merits of the decision. This was important to put across,

> especially where the subject matter of the case excites fierce controversy, the clash of wholly irreconcilable but deeply held views, and acrimonious, but principled debate.[26]

In the Court of Appeal, Sir Thomas Bingham, master of the rolls, took pains to emphasise the point. 'The court', he began,[27]

> has no role whatever as an arbiter between those who condemn hunting as barbaric and cruel and those who support it as a traditional country sport more humane in its treatment of deer or foxes (as the case may be) than other methods of destruction such as shooting, snaring, poisoning or trapping.

A sense that it would be inappropriate to do so may explain, in some cases at least, the disinclination to add the literary allusion. Self-protection (not ordinarily thought of as a judicial 'virtue') is identifiable as a second possible explanation.

A tale involving T.W.H. Crosland (1868–1924), the literary critic, best known at one time for his book on the sonnet, carries a warning for the occupant of the judicial bench tempted in an unguarded moment to display his literary credentials. J.B. Booth in his *London town* of 1929 relates the yarn. 'In the course of

25 1920 SC 805. **26** *R. v. Somerset County Council, ex parte Fewings* [1995] 1 All ER 513 at 515. **27** [1995] 3 All ER 20 at 24.

one of [Crosland's] innumerable libel actions', Booth commences his account,[28] an action

> tried before a judge of somewhat precious literary tastes, and somewhat of a pedant and poseur in addition, who had been at no pains to conceal his distaste for the uncouth figure in the witness-box, counsel quoted some lines from a sonnet. (Discreet counsel invariably assumed a literary tinge before this particular ornament of the bench.)
>
> 'What singularly beautiful lines, Mr ——,' purred his lordship approvingly, 'yet I can't recall them. Who wrote them?'
>
> And Tommy Crosland, lounging awkwardly in the witness box, with a Mephistophelian leer on his face, replied in his broadest Yorkshire:
>
> 'Ah did, me lord!'
>
> Whereupon the spoilt darling on the bench flushed a testy pink, and snapped a direction to 'get on with the examination'!

It would have to be conceded that literary quotation and literary allusion alike are but infrequently encountered by the reader of judgments of the judges raised in the traditions of the Common Law. But they are to be found, and there is little sign as yet of any pronounced judicial inclination to dismiss such embellishments in the reasoning of the courts as, in general terms, professionally inappropriate or unworthy affectation. It is true that in some instances the allusion is strained or the quotation of dubious relevance, but, in the majority of the examples included in the present compendium it is believed the justification for the allusion or quotation is self-evident: they point in the direction of the judicial decision that is being arrived at or, at the very least, furnish a supporting buttress for it. What is amiss with resort to a strategy of this sort in seeking to persuade the doubter?

Any listing of literary quotations and allusions in the judgments of the courts will necessarily be incomplete. The capacity of any one individual to cover the ground – to read all the reasoned judgments available in printed reports where literary quotations may indeed lie hidden – simply does not exist. The selection included here is based on reasonably extensive reading in the law reports even so. The bias, it will be immediately apparent, is in the pronouncements of judicial officeholders in Ireland, a bias that I trust will be excused in the case of a compiler who happens to have taught law in three Irish universities in the course of his academic career.

28 J.B. Booth, *London town* (London, 1929), pp 130–1.

Surprises await the adventurer who proceeds beyond these preliminary paragraphs. Who would have thought that Sir Edward Coke knew his Martial as well as he plainly did, or that irascible Irish lord justice of appeal, Jonathan Christian, his Aesop's fables? To raise such questions is, of course, to beg another: was the existence of the pertinent quotation or allusion present in the mind of the judge as he listened to counsel's advocacy? Or did they come into his head at a later stage? Or is it the case that counsel in his argument made tactical use of them?

Baron Dowse of the Irish Exchequer court would, I sense, carry off the *palme d'or* for the most intelligent reworking of a literary reference – one drawn from Shakespeare – in the course of his judgment in *Dolan v. Kavanagh* in 1876.[29] The Scots judge Lord Anderson's judgment in the *Rothfield* case decided in 1920[30] would win a consolation prize for the multiplicity of literary references it contains. The theme – the inn in history – naturally lent itself to this species of treatment, though not everyone would have recognised St Paul as a person familiar with taverns on the outskirts of Rome. Lord Anderson was reversed on appeal but this high point in judicial decision composition does invite the comparison we have earlier drawn with the case-law focusing on deerhunting and foxhunting, where literary references we discovered were to be non-existent.

It is very probable that, with the decline in the study of the classics, future members of the bench are unlikely to regale us with apt quotations from Virgil, Martial or Juvenal. Hesiod, too (remarkably recalled in the *Westby Minors* case[31] that has associations with the premises – Roebuck Castle – now occupied by the Law School of University College, Dublin),[32] amongst the writers in Greek, is unlikely to be revisited either. One cannot but regret the trend, if only that it would appear to entail that in no future judgment are we likely to encounter another impeccable sentiment from the same Greek author:[33]

> γλώσσης τοι θησαυρὸς ἐν ἀνθρώποισιν ἄριστος
> Φειδωλῆς, πλείστη δὲ χάρις κατὰ μέτρον ἰούσης.
> Εἰ δε κακὸν εἴπῃς, τάχα κ'αὐτὸς μεῖξον ἀκούσαις.

> (The best treasure a man can have is a sparing tongue, and the greatest pleasure, one that moves orderly; for if you speak evil, you yourself will soon be worse spoken of.)

29 (1876) IR 10 CL 166. **30** *Rothfield v. North British Ry. Co.*, 1920 SC 805. **31** *In re Westby Minors (no. 2)* [1934] IR 311. **32** The Westby family lived in Roebuck Castle from late in the nineteenth century down to the 1940s. **33** Hesiod, *Works and days*, trans. H.G. Evelyn-White (Loeb Classical Lib., Cambridge, MA, 1959), pp 54–5 (lines 719–21).

Nor, for that matter, are we likely to make the acquaintance of Carfania, the wife of the Roman senator, Licinius Buccio, ever ready herself, so Valerius Maximus – not, admittedly, the most reliable of witnesses – would have us believe, for lawsuits (prompta ad lites contrahendas), not because she personally could not find lawyers to represent her but because she had too much time, immodestly so, on her hands:

> non quod advocatis deficiebatur, sed quod impudentia abundabat.[34]

More's, surely, the pity.

In the compendium that follows I have eschewed the temptation to include any literary fragments recalled in academic legal literature. The undertaking of any such survey would require the expenditure of gargantuan effort and must be left to others who might be tempted by the attractions of the enterprise. Some unusual discoveries are certainly likely to be made. A personal selection by the present writer would include G.H. Gordon's intriguing footnote on a singular problem in Scots criminal law to be found in his comprehensive monograph on that topic.[35] 'Indeed', Gordon wrote,[36]

> any attempt to discuss the Scots law of embezzlement leaves one in the state of mind described by T.S. Eliot in *Burnt Norton*: 'Words strain … Under the tension, slip, slide, perish. Decay with imprecision, will not stay in place, Will not stay still.'

34 Valerius Maximus, *Memorable doings and sayings*, ed. and trans. D.R. Shackleton Bailey, 2 vols (Loeb Classical Lib., Cambridge, MA and London, 2000), ii, 210–11 (bk. VIII. 3). **35** Gerald H. Gordon, *The criminal law of Scotland*, 2nd ed. (Edinburgh, 1978). **36** Ibid., p. 564, fn. 25.

CHAPTER 1

The Bible

GENESIS

In September 1718 Dr Middleton of Cambridge University sued in a university court Dr Richard Bentley for £4. 6*s*. Dr Bentley insisted that the process employed against him was illegal and unstatutable and refused to put in an appearance. At proceedings before the court held on 3 October, Bentley was held to be in contempt, and, according to university usage, as it was put, was deprived of his degrees – a BA, a BD and a DD. At a university congregation on 17 October, a special grace was propounded and approved which effectively confirmed that earlier decision. Bentley subsequently moved in the King's Bench for a mandamus to have restored to him these several degrees. Since he had been given no notice of the plan to deprive him of these degrees, the court was to hold that a mandamus must issue.[1] In his concurring judgment, Mr Justice Fortescue noted that 'the objection for want of notice can never be got over'.[2] 'The laws of God and man', he went on,

> both give the party an opportunity to make his defence, if he has any. I remember to have heard it observed by a very learned man upon such an occasion, that even God himself did not pass sentence upon Adam, before he was called upon to make his defence. Adam (says God) where art thou? Hast thou not eaten of the tree, whereof I commanded thee that thou shouldest not eat? And the same question was put to Eve also.[3]

*

In Glasgow in 1930 a shopkeeper called McGowan was prosecuted, under a section of the ponderously entitled Glasgow Corporation Order Confirmation Act of 1914[4] for the offence of keeping for sale indecent or obscene prints.[5] McGowan had exposed for sale in his shop window in London Road several miniature photographic prints of nude women. The fact that, as was apparently agreed on all sides, the photographs would not have generated the prosecutor's

1 *The King v. Chancellor, Masters and Scholars of University of Cambridge* (1723) 1 Str. 557, 93 ER 698. 2 1 Str. at 567, 93 ER at 704. 3 *Genesis* 3:9, 11, 13. 4 4 & 5 Geo. V, c. clxxviii, s. 21. 5 *McGowan v. Langmuir*, 1931 JC 10.

interest had they been displayed in a public art gallery, led the magistrate in the police court to state a case for the High Court of Justiciary, asking whether he had been right to convict. The High Court answered 'yes', though the lord justice-general, Lord Clyde, confessed to some doubt. The principal judgment in the High Court was delivered by Lord Sands. In a wide-ranging survey devoted to a history of standards of decency, Lord Sands was to introduce a predictable biblical precedent.[6] 'The most venerable record in history', he wrote,

> recognises that, while nakedness is innocent, shame comes with the consciousness of nakedness – 'They were both naked, the man and his wife, and were not ashamed ... and the eyes of them both were opened, and they knew that they were naked; and they sewed fig leaves together, and made themselves aprons.'[7]

Lord Sands was to add a further point:[8] 'The story of the sons of Noah shows that in certain circumstances' a veto on public exposure of certain parts of the human body to the gaze of others 'was not limited to exposure as between members of the opposite sex'.[9]

*

At the trial in British Guiana of one Lejzor Teper on a charge of maliciously and with intent to defraud setting fire to his own shop, evidence was given by a police constable that half an hour after the fire began he heard a woman's voice shouting, 'Your place burning and you going away from the fire'. Ordinarily, such evidence would have required to be excluded under the hearsay exclusionary rule, but different consequences would follow if the remarks could be regarded as forming part of the *res gestae*.

The Judicial Committee of the Privy Council was to allow Teper's appeal against conviction, on the grounds that the woman's remarks and the recounting of them by the police constable could not have formed part of the *res gestae*.[10] Lord Normand, in delivering the advice of the Board, touched on a related matter: the weight to be placed on any circumstantial evidence that had been adduced that Teper was guilty as charged.[11] His approach was studiously cautious. 'Circumstantial evidence', Lord Normand wrote,

> may sometimes be conclusive, but it must always be narrowly examined, if only because evidence of this kind may be fabricated to cast suspicion on

6 Ibid., at 14. 7 *Genesis* 2:25; 3:7. 8 1931 JC at 14. 9 *Genesis* 9:21–4. 10 *Lejzor Teper v. The Queen* [1952] AC 480. 11 [1952] AC at 489.

another. Joseph commanded the steward of his house, 'put my cup, the silver cup, in the sack's mouth of the youngest', and when the cup was found there Benjamin's brother too hastily assumed that he must have stolen it.[12] It is also necessary before drawing the inference of the accused's guilt from circumstantial evidence to be sure that there are no other co-existing circumstances which would weaken or destroy the inference.

LEVITICUS

Mr John Haley, who was blind, would daily choose to walk a short distance from his home in south-east London, using his white stick, to an omnibus stop where he would board a bus to take him to his place of work. On the street along which Mr Haley was accustomed to walk, the local electricity authority caused the digging of a trench 60 feet long lengthwise along the pavement. To guard the trench, at one end the workmen put a punner-hammer across the pavement with its long handle resting on some railings; and at the other end, a similar arrangement consisting of a pick and shovel. Notices too were displayed: 'Roadworks ahead'. On an October day in 1956, Mr Haley, walking along the pavement, tripped over the handle of the punner-hammer and fell. The result of the fall was that he became almost totally deaf. Mr Justice Marshall dismissed Mr Haley's claim in negligence and nuisance, a decision with which the Court of Appeal agreed.[13] The House of Lords, however, unanimously overturned the decision of the Court of Appeal, arguing that the electricity authority had been in breach of the duty of care appropriate in such a case.[14] Lord Guest in his speech in the House of Lords adverted to statistical evidence that the number of registered blind persons in the London area was 7,321 and that the proportion of blind persons for the whole of Great Britain was 'at the very least one in five hundred'.[15] No member of the Court of Appeal or of the House of Lords cited one apt quotation from the Bible, but Edward Terrell, QC, counsel for Mr Haley, did, in his argument in the unsuccessful appeal to the Court of Appeal[16] and again in the successful appeal to the House of Lords:[17]

> When Lord Atkin posed the famous question 'who is my neighbour?' in *Donoghue v. Stevenson*,[18] he was, of course, making a reference to the Mosaic Law. The House is reminded of another statement from the same source.

12 *Genesis* 44:4–13. 13 *Haley v. London Electricity Board* [1964] 2 QB 121. 14 [1965] AC 778. 15 Ibid. at 807. 16 See [1964] 2 QB at 123. 17 [1965] AC at 788. 18 [1932] AC 562.

The Third Book of Moses, Leviticus, Chapter 19, verse 14: 'Thou shalt not curse the deaf, nor put a stumbling-block before the blind.'

JUDGES

In two cases heard together in 1933, *Adair v. McGarry* and *Byrne v. HM Advocate*,[19] the High Court of Justiciary in Edinburgh (Lord Justice-General Clyde, Lord Justice-Clerk Alness and Lords Hunter, Sands and Martin) held, by a majority (Lord Hunter dissenting), that, at common law, the police were entitled, without a warrant, to take the finger-prints of a person apprehended on a criminal charge but not yet committed to prison. In one respect, Lord Hunter's dissent was no surprise, since regulations of 1904 made under statutory authority dating from 1891[20] enshrined a rather different rule for untried persons in prison, the latter not being liable to be 'measured' save by order of the Secretary of State for Scotland or upon a sheriff's or magistrate's warrant.

In a judgment concurring with the majority view,[21] Lord Sands examined the argument that taking fingerprints forcibly from a suspect breached the principle that no man was compelled to supply evidence against himself. The pronunciation test imposed on the Ephraimite in the book of *Judges* supplied an analogy which Lord Sands worked into his reasoning. 'Another argument which has been suggested',[22] the relevant passage in the judge's thinking commences,

> is that no man can be compelled to supply evidence against himself. Now, if the man voluntarily gives his finger-prints no question arises. The sole question relates to compulsion. If a man's finger-prints could not be obtained without some voluntary action on his part, and were to be obtained only by tormenting him until he agreed to give them, I could understand the argument. But, if, as I am led to believe, finger-prints can be obtained with very moderate force *nolens volens* of the patient, and if this is done when he refuses to give them, then there is a question of the man being compelled to supply evidence against himself. An Ephraimite who was compelled at the point of the Gileadite's sword to pronounce the word Shibboleth might perhaps have complained that he was compelled to incriminate himself. But not so the man whose finger-prints are forcibly taken. He is entirely passive, and he is not compelled to do anything requiring any exercise of his own will or control of his body.

19 1933 JC 72. 20 Regulations dated 20 August 1904, made under the Penal Servitude Act, 1891 (54 & 55 Vict., c. 69), s. 8. 21 1933 JC at 87–9. 22 Ibid.

Fleeing from their pursuers, Jepthah and the Gileadites, the Ephraimites faced a challenge at the ford of the Jordan.[23] Asked to pronounce the word 'shibboleth' (meaning, apparently, ear of wheat, stream or flood), the Ephraimites could only respond with 'sibboleth'.[24] This fatal mispronunciation identified them as the enemy.

A single Ephraimite, as Lord Sands chose to recall, had sought to run the gauntlet. His failure of the test had devastating consequences:[25]

> Then they took him, and slew him at the passage of Jordan: and there fell at that time of the Ephraimites forty and two thousand.

How exactly 'shibboleth', a test word, became over time, as Brewer phrases it,[26] 'a catchword or principle to which members of a group adhere long after its original significance has ceased' and 'hence a worn-out or discredited doctrine' is not immediately apparent.

JOB

In the disquisition on the meaning of the word 'spes', usually translated as 'hope', included by Mr G. Turner, QC in his argument before the Privy Council in the *Gorham* appeal (*Gorham v. Bishop of Exeter*),[27] council was to furnish a number of quotations from secular as well as other sources to demonstrate that 'spes' necessarily conveyed merely an expectation and never a certainty. These illustrations occurred in the context of the discussion of the 'hope' for resurrection in the burial service and of the 'hope' for spiritual generation in baptism[28] (see further the entry below, p. 41, on SALLUST). The one biblical source specifically alluded to comes from chapter 14 of the book of *Job*. This chapter starts with one well-known resounding declaration in the Authorized Version:[29]

> Man that is born of a woman is of few days, and full of trouble.
>
> He cometh forth like a flower, and is cut down: he fleeth also as a shadow, and continueth not.

23 *Judges* 12:1–5. 24 Ibid., *v.* 6. 25 Ibid. 26 *Brewer's dictionary of phrase and fable*, revised Ivor H. Evans (London, 1975), p. 993. 27 (1849–50) 89 RR 725. 28 At the heart of the doctrinal problem the focus of attention in the bishop's refusal to admit Gorham to his new parish of Brampford Speke. 29 *Job* 14:1 and 2.

Arguably, the mood becomes a little more optimistic once verse 7 of the same chapter is reached. This is the verse called in aid by Mr Turner for his interpretative footnote in the course of the argument in the *Gorham* appeal:[30]

> For there is hope of a tree, if it be cut down, that it will sprout again, and that the tender branch thereof will not cease.

ECCLESIASTES

Mr Justice Buckley, in his judgment for the Restrictive Practices Court in 1962 on the Net Book Agreement,[31] found time to respond to the argument prepared on behalf of the Registrar by Mr H.A.P. Fisher, QC that perhaps it would be no harm if some booksellers went to the wall since too many books were being published anyway. The judge responded as follows:[32]

> Prolificacy has been recognised as an ineradicable characteristic of writers at least since the day of the author of *Ecclesiastes* and, no doubt, for much longer. The world might not be a worse place if some books went unpublished but this court is not a censor of literary taste.

The reference to *Ecclesiastes* was, presumably, a reference to verse 12 in the last chapter, chapter 12:

> And further, by these, my son, be admonished: of making many books there is no end; and much study is a weariness of the flesh.

ISAIAH

McInerney v. Clareman Printing and Publishing Co.[33] was a defamation action brought in the early 1900s by an auctioneer from Ennistymon, Co. Clare. A Dublin special jury was to hold that the publishers of *The Clareman* had perpetrated no libel, but the Court of Appeal set aside that verdict and ordered a fresh trial. This second trial duly took place before Chief Baron Palles and another special jury, when McInerney was awarded £600 damages. Two allegations in

30 89 RR at 729 n. 31 *In re Net Book Agreement 1957* (1963) LR 3 RP 246, [1962] 1 WLR 1347. See further below, pp 98 and 105. 32 1 WLR at 1385. 33 [1903] 2 IR 347.

particular that had been published in the newspaper had rankled: that persons who had done business with the auctioneer lived in terror of their lives, and that the auctioneer himself was a 'land-grabber'. In his judgment in the Court of Appeal, Lord Justice Holmes went out of his way to exonerate the first trial judge, Mr Justice Gibson, from criticism that had been levelled at him for failing to explain to the special jury the possible meanings of the term 'land-grabber'. In the process he was to recall the first curse in a series of curses to be found in chapter 5 of the book of *Isaiah* and which immediately follow 'The song of the vineyard' in that chapter. 'Mr Justice Gibson was right', Lord Justice Holmes explained,[34]

> in not embarrassing the case with innuendoes. 'Land-grabbing' and a 'land-grabber' are familiar words to Irish ears; and their meaning is well understood. They imply that land is acquired by dishonest, discreditable or oppressive methods.

'The idea', he continued,

> is neither novel nor peculiar to this country. The 'woe' of the Hebrew prophet fell on those 'that join house to house, that lay field to field'.[35]

A second precedent follows, drawn from a comedy of the seventeenth-century English dramatist, Philip Massinger.

The full quotation from chapter 5 of *Isaiah*[36] is equally illuminating. The *Authorized Version* reads:

> Woe unto them that join house to house, that lay field to field, till there be no place, that they may be placed alone in the midst of the earth!
>
> In mine ears said the Lord of hosts. Of a truth many houses shall be desolate, even great and fair, without inhabitant.
>
> Yea, ten acres of vineyard shall yield one bath, and the seed of an homer shall yield an ephah.[37]

It is not thought that the immediately ensuing curse in *Isaiah* has been granted comparable judicial recognition, a lacuna some might wish to lament:

34 At 402. 35 *Isaiah* 5:8. 36 *Isaiah* 5:8–10. 37 'for ten acres of vineyard will yield only one barrel, and ten bushel of seed will yield only one bushel': the *New Jerusalem Bible*'s version.

> Woe unto them that rise up early in the morning, that they may follow strong drink; that continue until night, till wine inflame them!
> And the harp, and the viol, the tabret, and pipe, and wine, are in their feasts: but they regard not the work of the Lord, neither consider the operation of his hands.[38]

The very words from *Isaiah* quoted by Lord Justice Holmes, it is worth noting, are also rehearsed by Giraldus Cambrensis (1145/6–1223) in a remarkable paragraph in his *Journey through Wales*.[39] The Welsh of his day, Giraldus writes, were insatiable in their wicked desires:[40]

> We occupy each other's territory, we move boundary-fences, we invade each other's plots of land. Our market-places are piled high with goods for sale, and yet our courts are kept busy with legal cases, the palaces of our kings re-echo with complaints. This is what we read in Isaiah: 'Woe unto them that join house to house, that lay field to field, till there be no place, that they may be placed alone in the midst of the earth.'

DANIEL

In *Chudleigh's Case* in 1595[41] Chief Baron Periam found himself reflecting on the growth of uses, the predecessors of today's trusts. Uses, he was to observe, 'have extended themselves into many branches, and are to be resembled to Nebuchadnezzar's tree'.[42]

An explanation of sorts ensues, with a mixing of metaphors a bonus. 'In this tree', the chief baron continued,[43] 'the fowls of the air build their nests, and the nobles of this realm erect and establish their houses, and under this tree lie infinita pecora campi,[44] and great part of the copyholders and farmers of the land for shelter and safety'.

Tinkering with the use of anything more radical was ill-advised. If, the chief baron declared,[45] 'this tree should be felled or subverted, it would make a great print and impression in the land'. One way forward was intimated even so:[46]

38 *Isaiah* 5:11–12. 39 *Itinerarium Kambriae: The journey through Wales*, conveniently to be found in Gerald of Wales, *The journey through Wales and The description of Wales*, trans. and intro. by Lewis Thorpe (London, 1978). 40 *Journey through Wales*, op. cit., p. 103 (bk. 1, ch. 3). 41 1 Co. Rep. 113b, 76 ER 261. 42 1 Co. Rep. at 134b. 43 Ibid. 44 Countless herds of the field. 45 1 Co. Rep. at 134b. 46 Ibid.

'And therefore it was convenient to repress the mischief after by Parliament and not to have any retrospect to cases before'.

Nebuchadnezzar had seen his tree in a dream which Daniel was invited to interpret.[47] The interpretation did not make pleasant hearing. Nebuchadnezzar would be driven from his kingdom. And so it came to pass:[48]

> The same hour was the thing fulfilled upon Nebuchadnezzar: and he was driven from men, and did eat grass as oxen, and his body was wet with the dew of heaven, till his hairs were grown like an eagle's feathers and his nails like bird's claws.

Nebuchadnezzar, urged to pray and repent, did just that; and the outcome was his re-establishment in his kingdom.[49]

*

In the book of *Daniel*, Daniel secures the acquittal of Susanna, the wife of Joakim, on the charge of adultery brought against her by two elders.[50] Susanna was supposed to have had intercourse with a young man in her husband's garden. Joakim was a rich man and the garden, it is safe to assume, was of considerable size. Daniel responding to Susanna's protestations of innocence, and springing to her defence, was able to show that the elders, who had in fact lusted after Susanna themselves, and were the only witnesses, had in fact concocted their evidence. Interrogated separately, they were unable to agree as to the species of tree under which Susanna and her supposed lover were reckoned to have had sex. In the *New Jerusalem Bible* one elder is made to say the tree was an acacia, the second elder an aspen.[51] This disagreement on a point of little materiality was found persuasive, and Susanna in consequence was acquitted.

This episode features in a number of stories concerning defence counsel and their reputed success in the defence of their clients. Perhaps the most evocative of these yarns, most evocative since it introduces a welcome note of scepticism, is the one recounted by the nineteenth-century Irish barrister, John Adye Curran, KC who went on to become a county court judge.[52] There is no precise date but the episode Curran relates must have occurred in the late 1860s or early 1870s.

47 For the entire episode see *Daniel* 4. 48 *Daniel* 4:33. 49 *Daniel* 4:34–7. 50 *New Jerusalem Bible* (London, 1985), pp 1493–5: *Daniel* 13. 51 *Daniel* 13:54 and 58. 52 *Reminiscences of John Adye Curran K.C.* (London, 1915), p. 13.

> On one occasion [Curran writes in his memoirs],[53] I defended a prisoner before Chief Justice Whiteside. My defence was that the case for the prosecution was grounded on the concocted story of the two Crown witnesses, and I relied on contradiction, one by the other, in their evidence on facts not material to the issue. In my address to the jury I called their attention to the case of Susannah and the Elders, which, though not admitted by all to be part of the Scripture,[54] was at all events very ancient history. There the witnesses had, as here, been ordered out of court, with the result that, though agreeing in their concocted story, the Elders differed upon an apparently immaterial fact, the name of the tree under which the alleged offence had been committed, the result being the acquittal of the woman.

Now comes the note of scepticism, a note struck by the chief justice himself, as Curran brings his account of the episode to a conclusion. 'The Chief Justice, in charging the jury', Curran writes,[55]

> said that such argument could not apply in every case, as otherwise one might argue that the history of the crucifixion of Our Lord was false because the Gospels apparently differed as to whether both thieves were impenitent.
>
> At all events, the jury considered the case of Susannah was good enough for them, and acquitted the prisoner.

It needs to be remarked, en passant, that Whiteside's allusion to the Crucifixion is somewhat mysterious and possibly inappropriate (assuming Curran has reported him accurately). Three of the Gospels – Matthew, chapter 27, verses 38 and 44; Mark, chapter 15, verse 27; and John, chapter 19, verse 18 – are entirely silent as to whether the two 'thieves' ('bandits' or 'malefactors') crucified along with Jesus were 'penitent' or 'impenitent'. It is only in Luke's gospel – chapter 23, verses 39–43 – that we learn that one was and the other was not. In the *Authorized Version* we read as follows:

> And one of the malefactors which were hanged railed on him, saying, if thou be Christ, save thyself and us.
>
> And the other answering rebuked him, saying, Dost not thou fear God, seeing thou art in the same condemnation?

53 Ibid. 54 Like 'Bel and the dragon': *Daniel* 14 in the *New Jerusalem Bible*, the story of Susannah and the Elders counts as part of the Apocrypha and is omitted from the *Authorized Version*. 55 *Reminiscences of John Adye Curran K.C.*, p. 13.

And we indeed justly; for we receive the due reward of our deeds: but this man hath done nothing amiss.

And he said unto Jesus, Lord, remember me when thou comest into thy Kingdom.

And Jesus said unto him, Verily I say unto thee, Today shalt thou be with me in paradise.

Since three of the gospels say nothing at all as to whether the thieves were penitent or otherwise, it is hard to accept the supposed aptness of the comparison drawn by Whiteside.

MATTHEW

By a majority of 6–3, the United States Supreme Court, in 1929, reversed a decision of the 7th Circuit Court of Appeals to set aside an earlier District Court adjudication in Illinois to deny naturalisation to a Rosika Schwimmer.[56] Ms Schwimmer, born in Hungary in 1877 and a Hungarian citizen, came to the United States in 1921 to visit and to lecture. She applied for citizenship in 1926, only to be turned down over her answer to the question addressed to her in her application form as to whether she would be prepared to take up arms in defence of her new country. Ms Schwimmer claimed to be a pacifist and it was no surprise therefore when she wrote in the space provided: 'I would not take up arms personally'. For the Supreme Court majority this was a fatal admission. 'Whatever tends to lessen the willingness of citizens to discharge their duty to bear arms in the country's defence', Mr Justice Butler was to argue,[57]

> detracts from the strength and safety of the government. And their opinions and beliefs as well as their behavior indicating a disposition to hinder in the performance of that duty are subjects of inquiry under the statutory provisions governing naturalization and are of vital importance, for if all or a large number of citizens oppose such defense the 'good order and happiness' of the United States cannot long endure … The influence of conscientious objectors against the use of military force in defense of the principles of our government is apt to be more detrimental than their mere refusal to bear arms.

56 *United States v. Schwimmer* (1929) 279 U.S. 644. 57 279 U.S. at 650–1.

Ms Schwimmer was aged over 50, but that, according to Mr Justice Butler, made no difference:[58]

> The fact that, by reason of sex, age or other cause [conscientious objectors] may be unfit to serve, does not lessen their purpose or power to influence others.

Three justices – Brandeis, Sanford and Holmes – dissented, Mr Justice Holmes alone delivering a reasoned judgment.[59] That there was a place for pacifists amongst new citizens of the United States he had no doubt. Ms Schwimmer's answers on her form, he frankly conceded,[60]

> might excite popular prejudice, but if there is any principle of the Constitution that more imperatively calls for attachment than any other it is the principle of free thought – not free thought for those who agree with us but freedom for the thought that we hate. I think that we should adhere to that principle with regard to admission into, as well as life within, this country.

Strong language indeed, not likely, one senses, to attract too much support among the citizens of the United States today, traumatized as they have been by the attack on the World Trade Centre and the other catastrophic crashes of 11 September 2001.

In his peroration in the *Schwimmer* case, Mr Justice Holmes introduced a fresh consideration, pointing to the contribution made to the country of a religious group possessed of an outlook identical to that of Rosika Schwimmer:[61]

> Recurring to the opinion that bars this applicant's way, I would suggest that the Quakers have done their share to make the country what it is, that many citizens agree with the applicant's belief, and that I had not supposed hitherto that we regretted our inability to expel them because they believe more than some of us do in the teachings of the Sermon on the Mount.[62]

Particularly relevant in the present context was, of course, verse nine of chapter five in St Matthew's gospel: 'Blessed are the peacemakers: for they shall be called the children of God.'

Game, set and match?

58 Ibid., at 651. 59 279 U.S. at 653–5. 60 Ibid. at 654–5. 61 Ibid. at 655. 62 *Matthew* 5–7.

*

In 1921 Somerset County Council acquired Ower Stowey Customs Common, an area of some 148 acres possessed of a herd of red deer. At some point in the 1920s deerhunting started over the common led by the Quantock Stag Hounds. In the early 1990s a sub-committee of the county council made certain recommendations regarding management of the deer population, but the county council itself, in a dramatic move, voted by 26 votes to 22 to prohibit hunting on the common altogether. The ban was challenged successfully in proceedings before Mr Justice Laws,[63] and that ruling was upheld, albeit on a somewhat different basis, by a majority of the Court of Appeal, Sir Thomas Bingham, master of the rolls, and Lord Justice Swinton Thomas, Lord Justice Simon Brown dissenting.[64] At first instance Mr Justice Laws interpreted the salient clause in the Local Government Act of 1972 dealing with the powers of a local authority to mean that the county council was circumscribed in the exercise of its functions through being restricted to the adoption of measures exclusively directed to the better management of the lands in question. It was accordingly prohibited from taking decisions on moral grounds. Both Mr Justice Laws at first instance and Sir Thomas Bingham in the Court of Appeal were at some pains to point out that their concern as judges was not with the morality or otherwise of hunting as such but with the somewhat narrower issue of whether the county council were legally permitted to do what it had done. A line from St Matthew's gospel at the conclusion of that most difficult of parables, the parable of the labourers, was called in aid by Sir Thomas Bingham as he sought to make the legal position crystal-clear:[65]

> To the famous question asked by the owner of the vineyard: 'Is it not lawful for me to do what I will with mine own?' (Matthew, xx, 15) the modern answer would be clear: 'Yes, subject to such regulatory and other constraints as the law imposes.' But if the same question were posed by a local authority the answer would be different. It would be: 'No, it is not lawful for you to do anything save what the law expressly authorises. You enjoy no unfettered discretion. There are legal limits to every power you have.'

63 *R. v. Somerset C.C., ex p. Fewings* [1995] 1 All ER 513. 64 [1995] 3 All ER 20. 65 At 25.

MARK

In March 1967 one Arthur Craig was electrocuted while working at an electrically driven conveyor at his place of employment. This was the Hamilton Brickworks in Hamilton, Lanarkshire, where the works manager was a Mr Sinclair. There was evidence to support a possible claim for negligence, but the pursuers in the action that was commenced, Mr Craig's sister and two brothers whom he in part had maintained, could not mount a claim under that heading because of a ruling a century before in the *Eisten* case[66] that brothers and sisters of a deceased person could not sue for damages in an action based on the contention that negligence had caused the death of the deceased. The pursuers sought to avoid so major a legal obstacle by placing reliance instead on an action under the obsolescent doctrine of assythment.

The action under this heading was dismissed by the Second Division of the Court of Session, and, on appeal, by the House of Lords, successively.[67] In the House of Lords, the vote was split on whether the action of assythment still existed. But there was agreement that, even if the action itself was maintainable, in the circumstances disclosed it could not succeed. As it was put, in the absence of any averment that Mr Sinclair, the works manager at the brickworks, had been convicted of, or even charged with, any criminal offence, and that he had received, or would receive, if he paid assythment, i.e. compensation for the death, a pardon from the crown, the action was not competent, i.e. could not succeed.

The remedy of assythment went back to early days in the law of Scotland, and much time was spent both by the Second Division and by the House of Lords in seeking to explain its origins and its function. The sense of its primary purpose was well put by Lord Reid. 'From very early times', he wrote,[68]

> it was the law of Scotland, that, if a person was murdered his kindred could accept from the murderer, an assythment in money. It is not surprising that the early history is obscure, but it would seem probable that this was a means by which the murderer could buy off the vengeance of the kindred of his victim, and that in time assythment also came to regarded as a compensation to the kindred for the loss which they had sustained.

Lord Simon of Glaisdale found himself embroiled in matters of etymology as he, too, attempted to come to grips with the question of origins and functions.

66 *Eisten v. North British Railway Co.* (1870) 8 Macph. 980. 67 *McKendrick v. Sinclair*, 1972 SC (HL) 25. 68 1972 SC (HL) at 49–50.

Enlightenment of a kind, he maintained, was to be found in versions of the Bible. 'Contrary to the opinion of Lord President McNeil ...', he argued,[69]

> 'assythment' was itself at one time an English word (see the Oxford English Dictionary: Lord McNeil was going on Doctor Johnson). In its southern form of 'aseeth' it appeared in the 1388 edition of Wyclif's Bible: 'Pilat, willynge to make aseeth to the puple' (Mark, xv, 15) – a passage translated in the Authorised Version as 'willing to content the people', in the New English Bible as 'in his desire to satisfy the mob', and in the Jerusalem Bible as 'anxious to placate the crowd'. These various versions give the general senses of the word 'aseeth', 'asseth' or 'assyth' in Middle English. The usual idiom was 'to make (or do) asseth', derived from the Old French *fere asset*, itself from the Latin *satis facere*, meaning to satisfy (desires), to expiate (sins) or to make atonement (to a person for a wrong).

And Lord Simon was to conclude:[70]

> So far as I am capable of judging, the Scottish 'assyth' and 'assythment' had similar senses before becoming specifically legal terms.

The law reports contain a number of other discourses – one hesitates to dub them 'digressions' – on lexicographical problems. An Irish instance is afforded by Lord Justice Barry's foray into Latin usage in his judgment in *Agnew v. Belfast Banking Co. and Clancy* in 1896.[71]

A further word on Lord Simon's foray into English usage in *McKendrick v. Sinclair* is requisite. The verse from St Mark's gospel, which we are given in no less than four different translations, comes at that point in the story of Holy Week when Pilate, before whom Jesus has been brought for punishment, queries whether Jesus deserves to be punished at all. In the *Authorized Version*, Pilate asks:[72]

> What will ye then that I shall do unto him whom ye call the King of the Jews?

The chief priests, for their part, would brook no mercy:[73]

> And they cried out again, Crucify him.

69 Ibid., at 56. 70 Ibid. 71 [1896] 2 IR 204 at 223–5. See W.N Osborough, *Studies in Irish legal history* (Dublin, 1999), pp 41–4. 72 *Mark* 15:12. 73 Verse 13.

Pilate repeats his question:[74]

> Then Pilate said unto them, Why what evil hath he done?

There is no answer, just the repetition of their bloodthirsty demand. Pilate then yields to the mob, using the phrase featured in our etymological excursus over 'assythment', and the momentum that leads to the crucifixion then becomes unstoppable:[75]

> And so Pilate, willing to content the people, released Barabbas unto them, and delivered Jesus, when he had scourged him, to be crucified.
>
> And the soldiers led him away into the hall … And they clothed him with purple, and platted a crown of thorns, and put it about his head. And began to salute him, Hail, King of the Jews!

The Damages (Scotland) Act 1976[76] ended the legal uncertainty highlighted by *Mc Kendrick v. Sinclair*. It abolished outright the action of assythment.[77] At the same time, however, it extended to most relatives of any deceased killed in circumstances of negligence the right to maintain an action under that heading.[78] It thus set aside the doctrine adumbrated in *Eisten* which had caused Mr Craig's siblings in the first place to seek redress via the archaic remedy of the action of assythment.

LUKE

In *Donoghue v. Stevenson* a friend bought the appellant a bottle of ginger beer in a cafe in Paisley in Scotland. The bottle was made of dark opaque glass. The appellant was to claim for injuries she said she had suffered as a result of consuming part of the contents of the bottle which she was to maintain contained the decomposed remains of a snail. The lord ordinary was to hold that the averments in the case disclosed a good cause of action, but the Second Division of the Court of Session, by a majority, disagreed. The House of Lords, however, also by a majority, reversed the decision of the Second Division.[79] Thus, by virtue of this seminal decision in the law of torts, the manufacturer of an article of food, medicine or the like, sold by him to a distributor in circum-

74 Verse 14. 75 Verses 15–18. 76 1976, c. 13. 77 S. 8. 78 S. 1 and sch. 1. 79 *Donoghue v. Stevenson* [1932] AC 562.

stances which prevent the distributor or the ultimate purchaser or consumer from discovering by inspection any defect, is placed under a legal duty to the ultimate purchaser or consumer to take reasonable care that the article is free from any defect likely to cause injury to health. Lord Atkin's classic speech contains a celebrated passage, partly inspired by the parable in St Luke's gospel of the Good Samaritan.[80] 'The rule', this passage starts,[81]

> that you are to love your neighbour becomes in law, you must not injure your neighbour; and the lawyer's question, Who is my neighbour? receives a restricted reply. You must take reasonable care to avoid acts or omissions which you can reasonably foresee would be likely to injure your neighbour. Who, then, in law is my neighbour? The answer seems to be – persons who are so closely and directly affected by my act that I ought reasonably to have them in contemplation as being so affected when I am directing my mind to the acts or omissions which are called in question.

*

See further above, p. 21.

ACTS

There is a reference to the Acts of the Apostles in Lord Anderson's disquisition on the inn in history (see below, p. 55, under BOCCACCIO).

In the days of the Roman Empire, Lord Anderson was to write, 'something akin to the modern inn was established'. He went on: 'The brethren from Rome met Paul at "the Three Taverns".'[82]

80 *Luke* 10:25–37. 81 [1932] AC at 580. 82 *Acts* 28:15.

CHAPTER 2

Greece and Rome

HOMER
Homerus c. 900 BC

In *St Aubyn v. Attorney General* in 1951[1] the House of Lords wrestled with difficult wording in the Finance Act 1940[2] dealing with liability to estate duty. The taxpayer, Lord Radcliffe argued,[3] was entitled

> to be told with some reasonable certainty in what circumstances and under what conditions liability to tax is incurred or else to be told explicitly that the circumstances and conditions of liability are just those which the Commissioners of Inland Revenue in their administrative discretion may consider appropriate.

Turning to the specific problem before him, Lord Radcliffe proceeded to voice his criticism of the legislative provisions he was obliged to interpret:[4]

> The seventeen sections which constitute Part IV of the Finance Act, 1940, are expressed with what proves on investigation to be a vagueness so diffuse and so ambiguous that they may well produce in practice the second alternative while adopting in form the requirements of the first.

'This', he concluded, 'would be an unfortunate situation to have brought about'.

There then follows a pause for reflection which incorporates a reference to Homer, a reference destined to be pursued in more critical vein by a Scots judge two years later.

'The prayer of Ajax', Lord Radcliffe observed in *St Aubyn v. Attorney-General*[5] – Ἐν δὲ φάει καὶ ὄλεσσον –[6]

> has been heard before in your Lordships' House, but I think its appeal is even stronger when obscurity is created by deliberate legislation than when it arises from the less wilful confusions of the common law.

1 [1952] AC 15. 2 3 & 4 Geo. VI, c. 29. 3 [1952] AC at 44–5. 4 At 45. 5 Ibid. 6 *Iliad*, xvii, line 647.

Ajax's prayer to Zeus comes at a critical juncture in the Trojan War when Ajax and the other Greeks (the sons of Achaians) believed that Zeus had reversed the odds so as to favour the Trojans, not least because at the time a meteorological phenomenon – to be translated possibly, variously, as darkness, fog or a dust cloud – made it well-nigh impossible for the Greeks to launch a successful assault. Ajax's prayer is compressed into three lines:[7]

> Ζεῦ πάτερ, ἀλλὰ σὺ ῥῦσαι ὑπ' ἠέρος υἷας Ἀχαιῶν,
> ποίησον δ'αἴθρην, δος δ' οφθαλμοῖσιν ἰδέσθαι ·
> ἐν δὲ φάει καὶ ὄλεσσον, ἐπεί νύ τοι εὔαδεν οὔτως.
>
> (O father Zeus, deliver thou the sons of Achaians from the darkness, and make clear sky and vouchsafe sight unto our eyes. In the light be it that thou slayest us, since it is thy good pleasure that we die.)[8]

The sense of the short phrase ἐν δὲ φάει καὶ ὄλεσσον, as put into the lips of Lord Radcliffe's hardened professional advocate, must surely be: 'For heaven's sake make the law clear, even if the consequence is we lose our side of the battle'.[9]

A not entirely dissimilar problem, again involving a claim by the Revenue in respect of estate duty, came before the Second Division of the Court of Session (Lord Justice-Clerk Thomson and Lords Patrick and Mackintosh) less than two years later.[10] Lord Thomson in his judgment acknowledged that the earlier decision in the *St Aubyn* case had put beyond doubt 'the principles on which the words "thenceforward retained to the entire exclusion of the person who had the interest and of any benefit to him by contract or otherwise" [fell] to be construed'.[11] But, he continued, that did not really prove of assistance to the appellant in the instant case: 'the exhaustive and luminous treatment' of the topic in the *St Aubyn* case threw no light 'on the path to the solution of the present problem'.

Lord Radcliffe's summoning up of Ajax in support of his comments in *St Aubyn* invited, in the lord justice-clerk's opinion, a rejoinder culled again from Homer. Lord Radcliffe, Lord Thomson observed,[12] refers to the prayer of Ajax, but there was another occasion on which Athene answered the prayer of Odysseus, and Ajax had to confess,

7 *Iliad*, xvii, lines 645–7. 8 *The Iliad of Homer done into English prose by Andrew Lang, Walter Leaf and Ernest Myers* (London, 1883), p. 362. 9 Or, in Lord Dunedin's words in *Sorrell v. Smith* [1925] AC 700, at 717, where the appeal for guidance from the courts below recalled for him too Ajax's prayer: 'Reverse our judgment an it please you, but at least say something clear to help in the future.' See further R.E Megarry, *Miscellany at law: a diversion for lawyers and others* (London, 1955), p. 351. 10 *Thomas v. Inland Revenue*, 1953 Scots LT 119. 11 1953 Scots LT at 123. 12 Ibid.

ὢ πόποι,[13] ἦ μ' ἔβλαψε θεὰ πόδας[14]

(Damn! It was the goddess interfered with my running.)

The sense, I think, is that the tax-payer complainant has only himself to blame. Ajax's confession comes at the conclusion of a race between Odysseus, Antilochus and himself, which Odysseus had won. Ajax had been leading, but Athene had responded to Odysseus's prayer for help, by strengthening his performance and by placing ox dung in Ajax's path, which caused the latter to slip and slide. In addition, Ajax was handicapped by the noxious fumes – doubtless methane gas – given off by the dung. Or, as the Greek was to put it:

Ἀλλ' ὅτε δὴ τάχ' ἔμελλον ἐπαΐξασθαι ἄεθλον,
ἔνθ' Αἴας μὲν ὄλισθε θέων, βλάψεν γὰρ Ἀθήνη,
τῇ ῥα βοῶν κέχυτ' ὄνθος ἀποκταμένων ἐριμύκων,
οὓς ἐπὶ Πατρόκλῳ πέφνεν πόδας ὠκὺς Ἀχιλλεύς ·
'εν δ' ὄνθου βοέου πλῆτο στόμα τε ῥῖνάς τε.[15]

The race, of course, should have been re-run, but wasn't.

*

There is an apt allusion to the travails of Odysseus (Ulysses) in the Odyssey in the course of Lord Sands's extended discussion of the choice of criteria determinative of obscenity in the Scots case of *McGowan v. Langmuir* in 1931[16] (for the background, see above, p. 12). 'Standards [of decency]', Lord Sands was to claim,[17]

> have varied in different ages and they vary to-day in different countries ... There is nothing indecent in the human frame. Such a suggestion would be a libel upon nature. But ... while nakedness is innocent, shame comes with the consciousness of nakedness ...
>
> Except among some of the lowest savages the public exposure of certain parts of the human body to the gaze of members of the opposite sex has been regarded as indecent so far back as historical records extend. Even the wave-tossed and half-drowned Ulysses
>
> With his strong hand broke from a goodly tree
> A leafy bough that he might hide his shame[18]

13 The report in Scots L.T. prints πότσοι, plainly a mistake. 14 *Iliad*, xxiii, line 782. 15 *Iliad*, xxiii, lines 773–7. 16 *McGowan v. Langmuir*, 1931 JC 10. 17 Ibid., at 14. 18 *Odyssey*, vi, ll. 128–9.

before he ventured to approach fair Nausicaa and her maidens. Or, in the Greek,

> Ὣς εἰπὼν θάμνων ὑπεδύσετο δῖος Ὀδυσσεύς,
> ἐκ πυκινῆς δ᾽ ὕλης πτόρθον κλάσε χειρὶ παχείῃ
> φύλλων, ὡς ῥύσαιτο περὶ χροῒ μήδεα φωτός.

HESIOD
Hesiodus fl. 735 BC

The principal issue in *In re Westby Minors (no. 2)* in 1934[19] raised the question as to whether, in the exercise of the wardship jurisdiction, an Irish court could sanction, in the case of two minor children, who were also wards of court, their education outside the jurisdiction at schools in England. That this should occur accorded with the wishes of the family and others close to it: the children's two grandmothers, their mother, their aunt, godfathers and trustees. Chief Justice Kennedy held that the critical question in the case should be answered in the negative. But the Supreme Court, by a majority, set aside that decision and held that both Westby boys could continue to be educated in England. (This happened, though they were not to gain entrance to Harrow – what had been the family's preferred choice.) Speaking for the majority in the Supreme Court, Mr Justice FitzGibbon touched on a matter that also came up for consideration in the course of the original hearing and at the ensuing appeal: the excellence or otherwise of Protestant secondary schools in the then Irish Free State.[20] The passage in his judgment that tackles this theme merits extended quotation, not least on account of something quite rare in a modern Irish law report – a quotation in classical Greek. 'My knowledge of Irish Protestant schools', Mr Justice FitzGibbon begins,[21]

> is not confined to St Columba's College [in Dublin]. I was for many years a Governor of the Erasmus Smith's Schools, of which the Abbey School, Tipperary, was at one time in the front rank of Irish Protestant boarding schools, and I am still a Governor of the King's Hospital, a considerable secondary school.

Now comes the key argument:[22]

19 [1934] IR 311. 20 [1934] IR at 325–6. 21 [1934] IR at 326. 22 Ibid.

> Lack of adequate funds and endowments has always hampered the Irish schools and prevented them from providing equipment and means of education, to say nothing of the valuable scholarships and exhibitions, comparable to those afforded by the great English public schools.

The ancient saw

> Νῆ' ὀλίγην αἰνεῖν, μεγάλῃ δ'ἐνὶ φορτία θέσθαι,[23]

contains as good advice to-day, in the matter of educational institutions, as it did to Perses for his trading two thousand five hundred years ago.

(The Greek, taken from Hesiod's *Works and days*, may here be translated: 'Admire a small ship, but put your freight in a large one'.)[24]

Giving the complete passage in Hesiod furnishes an understanding of the context best:[25]

> But you, Perses, remember all works in their season, but sailing especially.
>
> Admire a small ship, but put your freight in a large one; for the greater the lading, the greater will be your piled gain, if only the winds will keep back your harmful gales.

Or, in the Greek:

> Τύνη δ', ὦ Πέρση, ἔργων μεμνημένος εἶναι
> ὡραίων πάντων, περὶ ναυτιλίης δὲ μάλιστα.
> νῆ' ὀλίγην αἰνεῖν, μεγάλη δ'ἐνὶ φορτία θέσθαι.
> μείζων μὲν φόρτος, μεῖζον δ'ἐπὶ κέρδει κέρδος
> ἐσσεται, εἴ κ' ἄνεμοί γε κακὰς ἀπέχωσιν ἀήτας.

AESOP

Aesopus fl. 570 BC

Dwyer v. Esmonde, reported at the level of the court of Exchequer and at that of the Court of Appeal,[26] was a libel action arising out of the eviction by the defendant landlord of the plaintiff from the latter's farm for non-payment of rent. Dwyer objected to the tone of a letter from Esmonde which had been published in the *Freeman's Journal* of 16 January 1877[27] in answer to an item

23 Hesiod, *Works and days*, line 643. 24 H.G. Evelyn-White's translation in the Loeb Classical Library ed. (Cambridge, MA, 1959), p. 51. 25 Hesiod, *Works and days*, ll. 641–4. 26 (1877) IR 11 CL 542; (1878) 2 LR Ir 243. 27 Reproduced: 2 LR Ir at 247–8.

appearing a few days earlier in the same newspaper, purporting to be an 'Address of the Kilkenny Tenant Farmers' Association to the Tenant Farmers of the County of Waterford',[28] and which likewise treated of relations between the two men. The letter to which Dwyer had taken umbrage accused him of forcibly re-entering the farm from which he had been evicted and sundry other matters including the intimidation of a third party whereby that party was deterred from becoming tenant of the now vacant farm. In Esmonde's view, the allegations made against him in the previously published address amounted to a series of false charges imputing gross misconduct and harshness to him as a landlord. Not least because he was a parliamentary candidate in Waterford, it was only right that he should have exercised a right of reply to set the record straight.

The Exchequer was to hold that not every point in Esmonde's letter could be viewed as privileged in the circumstances, and thus allowed a single demurrer.[29] The Court of Appeal unanimously overruled that adjudication, affirming both that Esmonde enjoyed a privilege to publish matter of vindication and defence in answer to the charges advanced by Dwyer and published in the Address and that all the statements contained in Esmonde's letter were sufficiently connected with and relevant to Dwyer's charges to bring them within the privilege.[30]

Among the members of the Court of Appeal, Lord Justice Christian made no secret of the interpretation he was prepared to place on the last paragraph of the published Address of the Kilkenny Tenant Farmers' Association. Its 'truculent suggestiveness' he considered concealed an incitement to murder.[31] Christian, in his unrevised judgment, introduced a literary allusion to make his meaning unmistakably clear as to the side in the dispute who had the best claim to the protection of justice. 'When I was told at the close of the argument', he went on,[32]

> that this veiled hinting at murder had found its way into the newspaper under the guise of a mere advertisement – as if that could be an excuse – I was forcibly reminded of that fable of Aesop's called 'The trumpeter taken prisoner'. The prisoner begged hard for quarter, on the ground that he was a harmless person who wore no arms, but only his trumpet, which he was obliged to sound at the word of command – just as we might imagine our journalist appealing to his judge and jury to the effect that he too was a harmless person who had done nothing but insert in the way of business an advertisement which he had paid for. But the answer he would get would

28 Reproduced: 2 LR Ir at 249–50. 29 (1877) IR 11 CL 542. 30 (1878) 2 LR Ir 243. 31 2 LR Ir at 263. 32 Ibid., 263–4.

> be probably the same which the trumpeter's captors gave to him. 'No', said they, 'for the very reason you have given, we are determined not to spare you; for, though you yourself never fight yet, with that wicked instrument of yours you blow up animosity between other people, and so become the occasion of much bloodshed'.

There are several versions of tales such as this one in the Aesopic canon, the reasons for which are admirably summarised in a recent edition by Laura Gibbs.[33] In a comparable fable, numbered 121 in Gibbs's edition,[34] the sole protagonists are the soldier and his trumpet. When the trumpet seeks to be excused from the fate the soldier was determined on meting out to all his weapons of war – being hurled into the flames of a fire – the soldier was unmoved. His reaction indeed recalled that of the trumpeter's captors in the version of the fable recounted by Lord Justice Christian: the trumpet, though superficially innocent, had urged on others to carry out deeds of wickedness.

HERODOTUS
484–?424 BC

There is a passing reference to the *Histories* of Herodotus in Lord Sands's survey of the history of obscenity in the Scots case of *McGowan v. Langmuir*[35] (for the background, see p. 12 above). 'Standards' [of decency], the judge was to aver, 'have varied in different ages, and they vary to-day in different countries. If I recollect aright, this observation is as old as Herodotus.'[36]

The reference here is almost certainly to the story Herodotus relates of Candaules, the tyrant of Sardis, Candaules's wife, and Gyges, the tyrant's bodyguard.[37] Candaules forces Gyges to view his wife naked so as to secure confirmation of his contention that she was the most beautiful of women. Candaules's wife notices that she had been seen naked, and by way of avenging this insult to her modesty and of revenging herself on her husband (who she rightly suspected had egged Gyges on) compels Gyges either to commit suicide or kill Candaules and seize both her as his wife and the kingdom. Gyges adopts the latter course. Gyges had originally entered a protest against what Candaules had urged him to do:[38]

33 *Aesop's Fables*, trans. with intro. and notes by Laura Gibbs (Oxford, 2002). 34 At p. 63. This fable is no. 39 in the Avianus text, *Avianus*, ed. J.W. Duff and A.M. Duff (Cambridge, MA, 1934); and no. 370 in Ben Perry's *Aesopica* (Urbana, IL, 1952). 35 1931 JC 10. 36 Ibid., at 14. 37 Herodotus, *Histories*, bk. 1, 7–13. 38 Ibid., bk. 1, 8.

When a woman takes off her clothes she puts away her claim to respect. The proprieties among human kind were settled in times gone by; and we must observe them.

ἅμα δὲ κιθῶνι ἐκδυομένῳ συνεκδύεται καὶ τὴν αἰδῶ γυνή · πάλαι δὲ τὰ καλὰ ἀνθρώποισι ἐξεύρηται, ἐκ τῶν μανθάνειν δεῖ · ἐν τοῖσι ἓν τόδε ἐστί, σκοπέειν τινὰ τὰ ἑωυτοῦ.

Self-evidently, and disastrously for him, Candaules belonged to a different school of thought.

EURIPIDES
480–406 BC

A line in Euripides's play *Hippolytus*, line 612 –

ἡ γλῶσσ' ὀμωμοχ', ἡ δὲ φρὴν ἀνώματος –

is credited with being the most celebrated line in all Greek classical drama.[39] The context in which the words are spoken, by none other than Hippolytus himself, is certainly remarkable, which may help to explain how the line has entered into universal consciousness, even to the extent of being referred to in a key judgment of the Irish High Court in 2005.

Hippolytus was the illegitimate son of Theseus, king of Athens, and Antiope, queen of the Amazons. Grown to manhood, Hippolytus lived a life of chastity, which annoyed Aphrodite, the goddess of love, who resolved to use her powers to occasion his death. The ploy resorted to was to cause Phaedra, Theseus's wife, to fall in love with Hippolytus, her step-son. Hippolytus spurned Phaedra's advances, whereupon Phaedra, still besotted with the young man, plans to destroy herself and Hippolytus too. She confides in her nurse her resolve to starve herself to death, whereupon the nurse, anxious if possible to avoid the impending tragedy, tells Hippolytus that his stepmother loves him, urging him to reciprocate, having first commanded him to swear an oath not to disclose any of this.[40] Hippolytus remains unmoved and Phaedra takes more drastic action. She hangs herself, having penned a note, inscribed on a tablet, that she was doing this because Hippolytus had raped her. Despite what was to happen, the nurse had urged Hippolytus not to break his oath:

39 Harry C. Avery, '"My tongue swore, but my mind is unsworn"', *Transactions of the American Philosophical Society*, xcix (1968), 19. 40 In Aristophanes's *The Frogs* a place in Hell was reserved for those who broke their oaths (lines 145–51).

ὦ τέκνον, ὅρκους μηδαμῶς ἀτιμάσῃς,[41]

to which Hippolytus responded in line 612 that, although his tongue had sworn that oath, his mind had remained unsworn. In short, he gave no guarantee that he would not. A diatribe against all women follows.

Following the discovery of Phaedra's note, Theseus jumps to the conclusion that Hippolytus is indeed guilty. Poseidon, the sea god (who in certain traditions is viewed as the father of Theseus), is then summoned up by Theseus to cause a horrific accident in which Hippolytus is fatally injured. A messenger reporting the news expresses the sentiment that one should never have believed Hippolytus guilty, not even if the whole of womankind had hanged themselves and written messages on tablets made from all the pine forests on Mount Ida –

οὐδ' εἰ γυναικῶν πᾶν κρεμασθείη γένος
καὶ τὴν ἐν Ἴδῃ γραμμάτων πλήσειέ τις
πεύκην.[42]

Father and son are eventually reconciled shortly before Hippolytus finally expires.

Curtin v. Houses of the Oireachtas[43] was an unsuccessful challenge by Judge Curtin to procedures intended to be employed by the Irish parliament to secure his removal from office. He had been acquitted on a charge of downloading child pornography following a ruling that the warrant authorising a search at his house had been spent. In the course of his judgment in the High Court, Mr Justice Smyth dwelt on the terms of the oath of office that Curtin had taken when he became a judge of the Circuit Court. The public, Mr Justice Smyth argued, expect judges to fulfil the terms of their oath of office. He went on: 'Euripides's Hippolytus "With tongue I swore it, but my mind's unsworn" would be anathema.'[44]

Racine's classic piece of theatre *Phèdre* revisits the story of Hippolytus. There is even an imaginative reworking in the second volume in Emile Zola's cycle of twenty novels, Les Rougon-Macquart: *La curée* (1872). Here the characters loosely based on those of Phaedra and Hippolytus, Rénee and Maxime respectively, actually attend a performance of Racine's *Phèdre* given in an Italian translation.[45]

Judge Curtin's appeal to the Supreme Court against the decision of Mr Justice

41 *Hippolytus*, line 611. 42 Ibid., lines 1252–4. 43 High Court, 4 May 2005. 44 *Curtin v. Houses of the Oireachtas*, pp 124–5. 45 *La curée*, ch. 6.

Smyth to deny him relief was unsuccessful.[46] The judge himself resigned from his post in November 2006, before the Joint Oireachtas Committee which had been charged to investigate the case and report had made significant progress.

PLATO
429/8–347 BC

See the first entry under CICERO, below.

CICERO
M. Tullius Cicero 106–43 BC

In his lengthy discussion in *Gilbert v. Buzzard*[47] of arrangements historically for the disposal of the bodies of the dead, Sir William Scott quotes two passages from Cicero's *De legibus*.

In Cicero's opinion, Scott tells us first,[48] the oldest method of burial of which there was record was that which, according to Xenophon, was utilised in the case of Cyrus:

> At mihi quidem antiquissimum sepulturae genus illud fuisse videtur, quo apud Xenophontem Cyrus utitur.[49]

Here the body was returned to the soil, and positioned and laid to rest as if its mother's covering were drawn over it:

> redditur enim terrae corpus et ita locatum ac situm quasi operimento matris obducitur.[50]

But there were constraints, as Cicero was to take pains to point out, and as Scott recalled.[51] Quoting Plato (*Laws*, XII, 958D, and not, as Scott mistakenly observes, Plato's *Republic*), Cicero claimed that land in cultivation or capable of cultivation was not to be used as a cemetery. Cicero continued,

46 *Curtin v. Dáil Eireann* [2006] 2 ILRM 99. 47 (1821) 2 Hag. Con. 333, 161 ER 761. 48 2 Hag. Con. at 341, 161 ER at 764. 49 *De legibus*, II, xxii, 56. 50 Ibid. 51 2 Hag. Con. at 354–5, 161 ER at 769.

quae autem terra fruges ferre, et, ut mater, cibos suppeditare possit, eam ne quis nobis minuat neve vivus neve mortuus.[52]

But land proven capable of furnishing crops and of providing us with food like a mother should not be diminished in size by anyone, whether living or dead.

The relevant passage from Plato's *Laws* should be noted. No tombs, Plato argued, were to be put in places where man has tilled the soil, whether the monument be great or small:

τὰς θήκας δ' εἶναι τῶν χωρίων ὁπόσα μὲν ἐργάσιμα μηδαμοῦ, μήτε τι μέγα μήτε τι σμικρὸν μνηῖα, ἃ δὲ δὴ χωρία πρὸς τοῦτ' αὐτὸ μόνον φύσιν ἔχει, τὰ τῶν τετελευτηκότων σώματα μάλιστα ἀλυπήτως τοῖς ζῶσι δεχόμενα κρύπτειν, ταῦτα ἐκπληροῦν · τοῖς δε ἀνθρώποις ὅσα τροφὴν [μήτηρ οὖσα ἡ γῆ πρὸς ταῦτα] πέφυκε βούλεσθαι φέρειν, μήτε ζῶν μήτε τις ἀποθανὼν στερείτω τὸν ζῶνθ' ἡμῶν.[53]

*

Curtin v. Houses of the Oireachtas in 2005 was an unsuccessful challenge by Judge Curtin, a judge of the Irish Circuit Court, to procedures intended to be used by the Irish parliament to bring about the judge's removal from office.[54] For the background, see above, p. 37. In the course of his judgment in the High Court, Mr Justice Smyth dwelt on the duties of judges as a class, the expectations that the public understandably had of them. In the process, Mr Justice Smyth alluded to the discussion of the matter in Cicero's *De officiis*, remarking that, while Cicero's work was 'not a prescribed text for the behaviour of judges', it was certainly worth recalling that 'the limitations or restraints of public office' were 'not a feature of modern or contemporary times'.[55]

The passage Mr Justice Smyth appears to have had in mind was the following:

Est igitur proprium munus magistratus intellegere se gerere personam civitatis debereque eius dignitatem et decus sustinere, servare leges, iura discribere, ea fidei suae commissa meminisse.[56]

It specifically behoves the judge to remember that he represents the state, that it is his duty to sustain its honour and its dignity, to administer the law, to give everyone their due, bearing in mind that all this has been bestowed upon him as a sacred trust.

52 *De legibus*, II, xxvii, 67. 53 Plato, *Laws*, XII, 958, D–E. 54 High Court, 4 May 2005. 55 Ibid., at p. 125. 56 *De officiis*, bk. 1, xxxiv, 124.

LUCRETIUS

T. Lucretius Carus 95–*c.*51 BC

Lord Brougham was to dissent from his colleagues Lords Cottenham, Campbell and Denman, when the latter on the hearing of the writ of error, enabling an appeal to be brought in the case of Daniel O'Connell and others, in 1844, ordered that the judgment of the court below, the Irish Queen's Bench should be reversed.[57] The drama surrounding the events of what had been a major state trial at bar punctuates the earlier chapters of Anthony Trollope's novel, *The Kellys and the O'Kellys*.[58] Lord Brougham commences his speech with a lengthy justification of the practice then obtaining in the House of Lords of inviting the attendance of the common law judges to secure their opinion on the legal questions arising. The practice had been followed in the instant case, Brougham explained,[59]

> because the cause was one of great public importance: it was a government prosecution: it regarded an extensive conspiracy against the peace of the realm; above all, it was a political question, and one exciting great temporary interest among the parties which divide the country, and which also divide the two branches of the Legislature.

The common law judges were uniquely placed to offer impartial advice, Brougham contended, sitting as they did in

> courts from which are excluded all access to party feelings, whether of the one class or the other; and all bias, whether from popular influence or the authority of the executive power.

The eulogy of the entire bench reaches unaccustomed heights with Brougham capitalising on a few apt lines from Lucretius's *De rerum natura*. 'These judges', the House of Lords had called in to assist,[60]

> who are placed by their exalted position and unsullied character above any such vulgar control, who occupy unmoved and serene those elevated heights.

57 *O'Connell v. R.*, 11 Cl. & F. 155, 8 ER 1061. 58 Published 1848. 59 11 Cl. & F. at 327, 8 ER at 1126. 60 Ibid.

despicere unde queas alios passimque videre
errare, atque viam palanteis quaerere vitae.[61]

whence you can look down on other men and perceive them straying hither and thither as they seek the way through life.

There is, it may be remarked, more than a hint of Shakespeare in succeeding lines from Lucretius's poem:

O miseras hominum mentes, o pectora caeca!
qualibus in tenebris vitae quantisque periclis
degitur hoc aevi quodcumquest![62]

O pitiful minds of men, o blind hearts.
In such gloom of life, in such great dangers
is eked out your poor span of years.

SALLUST
C. Sallustius Crispus 86–34 BC

Rallying his forces for a planned seizure of power in the Rome of 63 BC, Catiline, in the speech attributed to him by Sallust, emphasised the point that they had nothing to lose, and everything to gain. Those in authority, he argued, were certainly enjoying the spoils of office. They, in contrast, had nothing, and there was no prospect of any improvement, at least not unless they were prepared to act: 'Things are bad, and we are faced with a still more hopeless future', or, in the Latin: 'Mala res, spes multo asperior'.[63]

It is this very Latin phrase that Mr Turner, QC, counsel for the Revd G.C. Gorham in the latter's celebrated appeal of 1850 to the Judicial Committee of the Privy Council, called in aid when discussing the doctrine of the Church of England in regard to infant baptism.[64] Gorham had been presented to the living of Brampford Speke in Devon, but the bishop of Exeter had refused to institute him on account of his views on baptism which the bishop regarded as unsound. Gorham had maintained, during an investigation of his beliefs that lasted five days, that 'spiritual regeneration was not conferred by baptism'. That, the bishop insisted, was not Church of England doctrine, and the dean of arches agreed

61 Lucretius, *De rerum natura*, II, 9–10. 62 Ibid., II, 14–16. 63 Sallust, *Cat.* 20.13 (and not, as in the report alluded to below, *Cat.* 13.20). 64 (1850) 14 Jur. 443, 89 RR 725.

when the matter was tested in court, so no order could go forth compelling the bishop to institute Gorham. The Judicial Committee of the Privy Council (the lord president, Lord Langdale, master of the rolls, Lord Campbell, Vice-Chancellor Knight-Bruce, Baron Parke, Sir S. Lushington, the Rt. Hon. T. Pemberton Leigh, the archbishop of Canterbury, the archbishop of York, the bishop of London), by a majority – Vice-Chancellor Knight-Bruce and the bishop of London disagreed – overturned the decision of the dean of arches. The bishop, they decided, had mistaken the doctrine of the Church of England. The headnote accompanying the report of the Privy Council's advice, a judgment delivered by Lord Langdale, admirably summarises the conclusions at which it had arrived:

> In the Church of England many points of theological doctrine have not been decided.
>
> The doctrines, that baptism is a sacrament generally necessary to salvation, but that the grace of regeneration does not so necessarily accompany the act of baptism that regeneration invariably takes place after baptism; that baptism is an effectual sign of grace, by which God works invisibly in us, but only in such as worthily receive it, in whom alone it has a wholesome effect; that, without reference to the qualification of the recipient, baptism is not in itself an effectual sign of grace; that infants baptised, and dying before actual sin, are certainly saved, but that in no case is regeneration in baptism unconditional – are not contrary or repugnant to the doctrine of the Church of England.

In pressing the Judicial Committee to adopt such a stance, Mr Turner alluded to another area of possible controversy where the doctrinal position rested on hope and not a certainty. In the Church of England burial service, these words were to be employed by the officiating clergyman at the graveside: 'We therefore commit his body to the ground, &c., in sure and certain hope of the resurrection to eternal life.'

At the time of the Reformation, the key writings on the significance of baptism had appeared in Latin, and the key word, Mr Turner insisted, was the word 'spes'. 'Spes' entailed hope, in the sense of expectation, but never certainty. Illustrations are then furnished – from Milton, the book of Job and, finally, from Sallust's account of Catiline's speech:[65] 'Mala res, spes multo asperior'.

65 89 RR at 729n.

VIRGIL
P. Virgilius Maro 70–20 BC

Collins v. Blantern, heard by the court of Common Pleas in 1767,[66] appeared a straightforward claim for the payment of a bond for £700 in the plaintiff's favour. It emerged, however, that the sum in question formed part of an agreement to stifle a prosecution for perjury, which, naturally, placed an entirely different complexion upon the claim. The court unanimously held that the bond was void ab initio and that the plaintiff could not therefore succeed. Chief Justice Wilmot did not mince his words. This was a contract, he declared,[67]

> to tempt a man to transgress the law, to do that which is injurious to the community; it is void by the common law ... You shall not stipulate for iniquity. All writers upon our law agree on this, no polluted hand shall touch the pure fountains of justice.

The explanation of the outcome concluded with the incorporation of a remark aimed at Aeneas's companions by the priestess at the entrance to Avernus in book 6 of the *Aeneid* (to remove them from sight of the sacrifices): 'Avaunt, ye that are uninitiated'.[68]

> Whoever is a party to an unlawful contract, if he hath once paid the money stipulated to be paid in pursuance thereof, he shall not have the help of a Court to fetch it back again; you shall not have a right of action when you come into a Court of Justice in this unclean manner to recover it back. Procul o, procul este, profani.[69]

*

Two suits were instituted, one in the Irish Chancery, the other in the English, for the administration of the assets of the deceased, one Sophia Evans. At the hearing of the Irish suit, the master of the rolls made an order restraining the executor, the Hon. H.W. Parnell, from proceeding with the English suit. At the resultant appeal,[70] the master's classification of an order directing the executor to file a discharge as a 'decree' – a critical adjudication under the pertinent rules

66 2 Wils KB 341, 95 ER 847. 67 2 Wils KB at 350. 68 Ibid. 69 *Aeneid*, vi, 258. Wilmot's punctuation differs. He gives: 'Procul! O procul este profani'. 70 *Parnell v. Parnell* (1858) 7 Ir. Ch. Rep. 322.

on civil procedure – was objected to on the grounds that the order had been made without proofs.[71] The protest of counsel for the executor was to include a reference to sharp practice in the legal system of the Underworld. 'Is it the practice of this Court', counsel demanded to know, 'to make a decree without proof?'[72] 'Such a course', they went on,

> was once attempted in a case of *Joly v. Walsh*.[73] But the late Master Henn refused to affirm the draft order; and in a note in the fold compared the practice to that of Rhadamanthus:
>
> > castigatque, auditque dolos subigitque fateri,
> > quae quis apud superos, furto laetatus inani,
> > distulit in seram commissa piacula mortem.[74]
>
> > Trying and chastising wrongdoers, forcing confessions
> > From any who, on earth, went gleefully undetected –
> > But uselessly, since they have only postponed till death their
> > atonement.[75]

There is, as it happens, further discussion of these lines of Virgil by Sir Edward Coke. In his *Institutes of the laws of England – third part*, 4th ed. (London, 1670), at p. 35, Coke wrote:

> And the poet in describing the iniquity of Radamanthus, that cruel Judge of Hell, saith:
> castigatque, auditque dolos, subigitque fateri.
> First, he punished before he heard, and when he had heard his denial, he compelled the party accused by torture to confess it. But far otherwise doth Almighty God proceed postquam reus diffamatus est. I. Vocat 2. Interrogat. 3. Judicat. [with marginal references to Luke 16.1,2 &c., and John 7.51].

*

Knudsen's Trustees v. Secretary of State for Scotland,[76] a case decided by the First Division of the Scots Court of Session (Lord President Clyde, Lords Carmont, Sorn and Guthrie) in 1961, was the culmination of a dispute in Argyllshire over

71 7 Ir. Ch. Rep. at 323. 72 Ibid. 73 Unreported. 74 Virgil, *Aeneid*, vi, lines 567–9. 75 C. Day Lewis's translation: *The Aeneid of Virgil* (London, 1961), p. 133. 76 1962 Scots LT 40.

the reorganization there of educational endowments. The particular controversy concerned a difficulty connected with a deed of trust executed by Sir Karl Fredrik Knudsen, a naturalised Norwegian shipping magnate and banker, in favour of pupils who had attended Kilmartin public school. In exercising his powers under the Education (Scotland) Act 1946[77] to reorganize an educational trust, the Secretary of State for Scotland had to have regard 'to the spirit of the founders' of the trust.[78] In holding that, for the third time in the particular case, the secretary of state had failed to observe this requirement, Lord Guthrie, in a concurring judgment, quoted the passage in the *Aeneid* where Aeneas attempted unsuccessfully to lay hold of the spirit of his father Anchises.[79] It was an argument by analogy: the secretary of state had been equally unsuccessful in capturing the essence of Sir Karl Fredrik Knudsen's endowment. 'Virgil long ago', Lord Guthrie ruminated,[80] described in immortal lines the difficulty of grasping a spirit:

> Ter conatus ibi collo dare bracchia circum,
> Ter frustra comprensa manus effugit imago,
> Par levibus ventis volucrique simillima somno.
>
> (Thrice with his arms he essayed the beloved one's neck to embrace;
> Thrice grasped vainly, the phantom eluded his hands in flight,
> Thin as the idle breezes, and like some dream of the night.)[81]

Lord Guthrie drew the inevitable conclusion:[82]

> In the present case, I am afraid that the spirit of the intention of the truster has thrice eluded the Secretary of State, just as the spirit of pater Anchises thrice evaded the embrace of Aeneas.[83]

HORACE

Q. Horatius Flaccus 65–8 BC

Following incidents reported as having taken place during the general election of 1857, the House of Commons ordered the prosecution for intimidation of the

77 9 & 10 Geo. VI, c. 72. 78 Ibid., s. 116 (2). 79 *Aeneid*, vi, lines 700–3. 80 1962 Scots LT at 45. 81 The translation is acknowledged by Lord Guthrie to have been that of Lord Justice Bowen: Charles Bowen, *Virgil in English verse: Eclogues and Aeneid I–VI* (London, 1887), pp 295–6. 82 1962 Scots LT at 45. 83 The case and the classical erudition on display are both highlighted by W.A. Wilson in his *Introductory essays on Scots law* (Edinburgh, 1978), at pp 16–17.

Revd Peter Conway, the Roman Catholic curate at Castlebar, Co. Mayo. Conway's trial should have gone ahead at the Mayo assizes, but the Irish law officers, apprised of the state of local feeling, deemed it prudent to have the venue switched to Dublin. An application in that behalf was made to the court of Queen's Bench in Dublin, and the application was granted.[84] Supporting that decision, Mr Justice Crampton nonetheless went out of his way to emphasise the independence of the judicial bench. The atmosphere of the times undoubtedly explained resort to this unusual tactic. 'We shall fearlessly discharge our sworn duty', Mr Justice Crampton remarked, 'equally regardless of popular applause and of the fear or favour of the Crown.'[85] Three well-known lines of Horace were recalled:

> non civium ardor prava jubentium,
> non vultus instantis tyranni
> mente quatit solida.[86]

> [The judge] is not shaken from his firm resolve by the frenzy of his fellow citizens urging what is wrong, nor by the face of the threatening tyrant.

*

There is a reference to Horace in Lord Anderson's elegant essay on the inn in history (see below, p. 55, under BOCCACCIO).

In the days of the Roman Empire, Lord Anderson was to write, 'something akin to the modern inn was established':[87]

> The brethren from Rome met Paul at the Three Taverns (Acts, xxviii, *v.* 15). In Horace's interesting account of his journey from Rome to Brundisium, he refers to the inns he slept at in the course of that journey (*Sat.* i. 5).

Horace begins satire 5 in book 1 thus:[88]

> Egressum magna me accepit Aricia Roma
> hospitio modico; rhetor comes Heliodorus,
> Graecorum longe doctissimus: inde Forum Appi,
> differtum nautis, cauponibus atque malignis.

84 *The Queen v. Conway* (1858) 7 ICLR 507. 85 7 ICLR at 524. 86 *Carmina*, iii, 3, 2–4. 87 *Rothfield v. North British Ry. Co.*, 1920 SC 805 at 816. 88 Horace, *Sat.*, i, 5, lines 1–4.

Or:[89]

> Leaving mighty Rome, I found shelter in a modest inn at Aricia, having for companion Heliodorus the rhetorician, far most learned of all Greeks. Next came Appii Forum, crammed with boatmen and stingy tavern-keepers.

Horace's satire, it is believed,[90] was modelled on one by Lucilius, who in his third book had described a journey from Rome to Capua and thence on to the straits of Messina.[91] Here, too, one of the inns patronised by our traveller had little to commend it: he contracted a tummy upset and the food was deficient anyway ('ostrea nulla fuit, non purpura, nulla peloris/asparagi nulli'[92] – no oysters, clams or mussels, and no asparagus either).

SENECA
L. Annaeus Seneca c. 1 BC–65 AD

In *Maunsell v. Minister for Education* in 1940,[93] Mr Justice Gavan Duffy in the Irish High Court concluded that the principles of natural justice had been breached when a national schoolteacher, about to be made redundant as a result of a reduction in the numbers of pupils attending the particular school, had been given no opportunity to object. To stress the pedigree of the legal rule it was his intention to call in aid, the judge recalled lines from Seneca's play *Medea*:

> qui statuit aliquid parte inaudita altera,
> aequum licit statuerit, haud aequus fuit.
>
> Whoever shall have given judgment, leaving one of the parties unheard, will not have acted justly, even if his judgment in fact does justice.[94]

It may be observed that apt as this quotation from Seneca may have been, the judge chose to overlook the context in which in the play Medea utters her protest to King Creon that she has been unfairly treated:[95]

89 H.R. Fairclough's translation: Loeb Classical Library ed. (Cambridge, MA, 1978), p. 65. 90 Ibid., p. 62. 91 Lucilius, *Satires*, tome 1 (livres I–VIII) (Paris, 1978), pp 117–31. 92 Livre III, 28–30. 93 [1940] IR 213. 94 Lines 199–200 (amended from the judge's version). 95 For this passage see 'Roman law in Ireland', in my *Studies in Irish legal history* (Dublin, 1999), at p. 34.

Jason, her husband, had deserted Medea and was about to marry Creon's daughter, Creusa. Creon, anticipating (with some justification) great mischief on Medea's part, had ordered her instant banishment – the decision to which Medea had demurred in the lines reproduced in *Maunsell*. Jason intercedes. Creon relents, the sentence of banishment is deferred for 24 hours. Medea has now been given both the chance and the time to wreak her revenge. It is terrible indeed. First to die, as a result of Medea's machinations, are Creusa – Jason's intended bride – and King Creon himself. Also fated to die, again at Medea's hands, in the episode horrifically recaptured in Géricault's famous painting, are her two infant sons by Jason.

This was by no means the first occasion upon which these words in Seneca's *Medea* had been incorporated in a judgment of the court. In *Boswel's case* in 1606,[96] Coke cites the passage in a judgment where the King's Bench emphasised that no incumbent of a parish could be removed on a quare impedit or an assize of darrein presentment unless he was named in the writ.[97]

Five years later, Coke repeated the quotation in a case where one James Bagg, a burgess of Portsmouth, had been disenfranchised in what was considered an objectionable summary fashion.[98] Bagg had insulted Robert Trelawny, a former mayor, by calling him 'a cozening knave', and Thomas Fowens, the current mayor, by calling him 'an insolent fellow', following this up 'scoffingly, contemptuously, and uncivilly, with a loud voice … [uttering] these words … that is to say, ("Come and kiss")'.[99] Though the court held the corporation had been entitled to take action against Bagg, it was fatal that they had proceeded against him without hearing him answer to what had been objected and that he had not been reasonably warned.[1]

MARTIAL

M. Valerius Martialis c. 40–104 AD

Telling use was to be made of Martial's two lines on the swan in his *Epigrams* (Book XIII, The Xenia), in Sir Edward Coke's report of *The Case of Swans*.[2] This lawsuit, brought by the crown, against Lady Joan Young and Thomas Saunger, concerned the ownership of swans in the county of Dorset. Coke's

96 6 Co. Rep. 48b, 77 ER 326. 97 6 Co. Rep. at 52a, 77 ER at 331. 98 *Bagg's Case* (1615) 11 Co. Rep. 93b, 77 ER 1271. 99 11 Co. Rep. at 95a, 95b, 77 ER at 1274, 1275. 1 11 Co. Rep. at 99a, 77 ER at 1280. 2 7 Co. Rep. 15b, 77 ER 435.

report examines at length what on occasion could prove a vexed question – ownership in individual swans. The starting-point was the rule of common law that designated the swan a royal fowl. Such ownership inhered in the royal prerogative. The crown could, however, alienate its rights by conferring ownership in swans on a subject. Such grant would be commonly evidenced through the practice of marking individual swans in a particular way. In *The Case of Swans* the contention was advanced that the subject might enjoy under grant and by prescription the right to treat as his own all wild swans that were not marked and that built their nests, bred and frequented within a particular stretch of water. This contention was not accepted. Coke's report also touches on the problem of ownership of cygnets born to a cob and a pen 'owned' by two different persons.[3] It is at this point that Martial's verses are introduced, not, it would have to be said, in the most relevant of asides. The rule of law – that ownership of the cygnets should be divided equally between the two separate owners of the cob and the pen – was founded, Coke avers,

> on a reason in nature, for the cock is an emblem or representation of an affectionate and true husband to his wife above all other fowls; for the cock holdeth himself to one female only, and for this cause nature hath conferred on him a gift beyond all others; that is, to die so joyfully, that he sings sweetly when he dies; upon which, the poet saith:
>
> Dulcia defecta modulatur carmina lingua,
> cantator, cygnus, funeris ipse sui.[4]
>
> With weakened tongue, the swan, which chants of its own
> death, modulates sweet songs.[5]

Cicero, borrowing from Plato,[6] was to echo the same belief in his *Tusculan disputations*. Socrates relates, Cicero there recalls,

> ut cygni, qui non sine causa Apollini dicati sint sed quod ab et divinationem habere videantur, qua providentes quid in morte boni sit cum cantu et voluptate moriantur, sic omnibus bonis et doctis esse faciendum.[7]
>
> that just as the swans – who have been consecrated to Apollo, not undesignedly, but because from Apollo they seem to have the gift of prophecy,

3 7 Co. Rep. at 17a, 77 ER 437. 4 Martial, *Epigrams*, bk. 13, 77. 5 As translated by Leary, see fn. 12 below. 6 *Phaedo*, 84E. 7 *Tusculan disputations*, I, xxx, 73.

> and thus have a foretaste of the blessing death brings – die with a song of rapture, so must all good and learned men do likewise.[8]

Brewer's *Dictionary of phrase and fable* rubbishes the idea that dying swans sang at all, let alone sang sweetly: 'The fable that the swan sings beautifully just before it dies is very ancient, but baseless.'[9] Pliny, too was dismissive:[10]

> Olorum morte narratur flebelis cantus, falso, ut arbitror aliquot experimentis. idem mutua carne vescunter inter se.

> A story is told about the mournful song of swans at their death – a false story as I judge on the strength of a certain number of experiences. Swans are cannibals, and eat one another's flesh.[11]

The most recent commentator on Book XIII of *The Epigrams*, T.J. Leary, however, was to protest that grounds existed for so ancient a belief and these still obtain.[12] W.G. Arnott, cited by Leary,[13] made use of zoological data:

> The whooper [swan] … has a remarkably shaped trachea, convoluted inside its breastbone; and when it dies, the final expiration of air from its collapsing lungs produces a 'wailing flute-like sound given out quite slowly'.

TACITUS

C. Cornelius Tacitus c. 61–*c.* 117 AD

In 1868 no less than 5,346 women in Manchester sought inclusion in the register of voters. The revising barrister, in a test case, denied one Mary Abbott that right – a decision that was upheld on appeal by the court of Common Pleas (Lord Chief Justice Bovill, Mr Justice Willes, Mr Justice Byles and Mr Justice Keating): *Chorlton v. Lings*.[14] In a contemporary adjudication the Court of Session in Scotland had reached an identical conclusion: *Brown v. Ingram*.[15]

Mr Justice Willes's judgment in the English case is remarkable for its brief survey of the rights of women under the common law to be involved in the

8 Trans. J.E. King: Cicero, *Tusculan disputations* (Loeb Classical Library, London and Cambridge, MA, 1966), pp 85–7. 9 *Brewer's dictionary of phrase and fable*, revised I.H. Evans (London, 1975), p. 1050. 10 *Naturalis historia*, 10, 32. 11 Trans. H. Rackham: Pliny, *Natural history*, vol. 3: books 8–11 (Loeb Classical Library, Cambridge, MA, 1956), p. 333. 12 *Martial Book XIII: The Xenia*, text with intro. and commentary by T.J. Leary (London, 2001). 13 'Swan songs', *Greece and Rome* (2nd series), xxiv (1977), 149 at 152; *Martial Book XIII: The Xenia*, p. 136. 14 (1868) LR 4 CP 374. 15 (1868) 7 Macph. 281.

management of public affairs.[16] Willes remarks that whatever had been the position among the ancient Britons, things were arranged very differently among the Saxons. No one took part in the councils of the Saxons, Willes records, 'unless entitled to bear arms and invested with them in the public assembly, which investiture', he goes on, 'Tacitus likened to the assumption of the toga virilis'.[17] The appropriate citation from Tacitus, from his *Germania*, is given as a footnote:[18]

> Nihil autem neque publicae neque privatae rei nisi armati agunt. sed arma sumere non ante cuiquam moris, quam civitas suffecturum probaverit. tum in ipso concilio vel principum aliquis vel pater vel propinqui scuto frameaque juvenem ornant: haec apud illos toga, hic primus iuventae honos; ante hoc domus pars videntur, mox rei publicae.

> They transact no business, public or private, without being armed. But it is a rule that no one shall carry arms until the state authorities are satisfied that he will be competent to use them. Then, in the presence of the Assembly, either one of the chiefs or the young man's father or some other relative presents him with a shield and a spear. These, among the Germans, are the equivalent of the man's toga with us – the first distinction publicly conferred upon a youth, who now ceases to rank merely as a member of a household and becomes a citizen.[19]

JUVENAL
Decimus Junius Juvenalis fl. end of 1st century AD

In *Gilbert v. Buzzard*,[20] Sir William Scott found himself pondering the etymology of the word 'coffin', inevitably so in a case concerned with the right claimed by a husband, in order to defeat the machinations of the resurrection men, to bury his recently deceased wife in a lead coffin. Scott considered the origin of the word to lie in the Greek and Latin words for basket (κόφινος; cophinus), and quoted a passage from Juvenal's third satire to press home his

16 LR 4 CP at 388–90. 17 Ibid., at 389. 18 Tacitus, *Germania*, ch. 13. 19 Tacitus, *The Agricola and the Germania*, trans. H. Mattingly, revised S.A. Handford (London, 1970), p. 112. On the forlorn endeavour of the SS to seize the Codex Aesinas of the *Germania* in Italy during World War II and secure it for Hitler and the Fatherland, see Simon Schama, *Landscape and memory* (London, 1995), pp 75–81. 20 (1821) 2 Hag. Con. 333, 161 ER 761.

contention as regards the Latin etymology.[21] Here Juvenal bewailed the changes that had occurred at the archway of the old Porta Capena on the Appian Way on the great south road out of Rome. Numa had once held his assignations at the place, but, Juvenal claims,

> nunc sacri fontis nemus et delubra locantur
> Iudaeis, quorum cophinus faenumque supellex,[22]

> now the sacred fountain and grove and shrine were rented out to Jews, who possess only a basket and a truss of hay.

The sense is certainly of someone trading in knick knacks of one sort or another, redolent of the stall that Silas Wegg kept close to Boffin's residence in the early chapters of Dickens's *Our mutual friend.*

*

As is recalled in the Introduction – and as is recounted in chapter 90 of Herman Melville's *Moby Dick* (1851) – there was to be litigation over a whale captured by mariners three miles off the north coast of Kent in 1829.[23] The whale had been found by the masters and crews of seven oyster smacks, who managed to fix a line to it before towing it to a beach at Whitstable. The resultant lawsuit dealt not with any rights of the mariners as salvors, as might perhaps have been anticipated, but rather with the vexed question of ownership of the whale itself.[24] In proceedings before Dr Phillimore in the court of Admiralty, it was held that ownership of the whale reposed in the then Lord Warden of the Cinque Ports (originally just the five Kent and Sussex seaports of Hastings, Sandwich, Dover, Romney and Hythe, but later much extended), no less a personage then the duke of Wellington. This outcome, too, we have previously rehearsed.

It is important to note that, at the hearing before Dr Phillimore, the king in his office of admiralty had presented a rival claim, maintaining that 'all royal fishes such as sturgeons, grampuses,[25] whales, porpoises, dolphins, riggs[26] and generally all other fishes of very large bulk or fatness' had been granted by the crown to its commissioners of admiralty. Dr Phillimore accepted that in general this was true but, having examined the patents of appointment to the office of

21 2 Hag. Con. at 342, 161 ER at 764. 22 Juvenal, *Satires*, III, 13–14. 23 Above, p. 2. 24 *Lord Warden and Admiral of the Cinque Ports v. H.M. in his office of Admiralty* (1831) 2 Hagg. 438, 166 ER 304. 25 A popular name for various kinds of whale; technically, though, just Risso's dolphin. 26 The name of a shallow-water shark found in the eastern Atlantic and the Mediterranean.

lord warden of the Cinque Ports, he was satisfied that a special entitlement to ownership of royal fish had been created in favour of the lord warden within his territorial jurisdiction. This was explicit in the case of patents from the time of William III and of Anne, and implicit in the case of the duke of Wellington's patent which bestowed upon him as lord warden 'all the commodities, emoluments, profits and perquisites, in as ample a manner as they have been granted to any of his predecessors.' In this key adjudication of *Lord Warden and the Admiral of the Cinque Ports v. H.M. in his office of Admiralty*, Dr Phillimore investigated the origin of the rule ordinarily applying that whales and sturgeons belonged to the crown and were thus royal fish. The sixteenth-century law reporter, Plowden, Herman Melville reminds us,[27] believed that the whale when caught belonged to the monarch 'because of its superior excellence' – an explanation which Melville understandably did not find particularly persuasive.[28] In the case of the whale beached at Whitstable, Dr Phillimore offered a different explanation, calling in aid for the purpose a line from Satire Four in Juvenal – a remarkable instance of intellectual sleight-of-hand. The whale, wrote Phillimore in his judgment,[29] 'is property so inherent in the Crown that, by a species of legal fiction, it is to be restored to the king as its rightful owner: *veterem ad dominum debere reverti*.[30]

The context in which Juvenal had occasion to examine a comparable legal problem merits a note. Satire Four concerns a gigantic turbot (*rhombus*) which had been netted in the Adriatic in front of the shrine of Venus at Ancona. It was to be sent to the emperor Domitian (81–96 AD) as a royal fish. Since it was too large for any cooking vessel to be found in the palace kitchen, Domitian, Juvenal would have us believe, summoned his cabinet to discuss how to deal with it. The last section of the satire is an extended parody aimed at Domitian, whom Juvenal of course had had reason to fear, and at the yes-men who composed his cabinet.[31] Early in the satire, Juvenal identified himself with the fishermen who had had the misfortune to trap this gigantic fish. Who would have dared, he asked, to put up for sale or to buy so huge a fish when the seashore teemed with informers (*cum plena et litora multo delatore forent*)? Inspectors of seaweed (*algae inquisitores*) would at once have pounced on any luckless mariner who dared to claim that the turbot had escaped from some royal fishpond. A fugitive from

27 *Moby Dick*, ch. 90: 'Heads or tails'. The chapter heading is accompanied by a quotation from Bracton. 28 'And', writes Melville, 'by the soundest commentators this has ever been held a cogent argument in such matters'. Ibid. 29 2 Hagg. at 441, 166 ER at 305. 30 Juvenal, *Satires*, IV, 52. 31 See generally Gilbert Highet, *Juvenal the satirist: a study* (Oxford, 1954), pp 76–82. Suetonius's portrait of Domitian may be compared: *De vita Caesarum*, liber VIII (*Suetonius*, trans. J.C. Rolfe, 2 vols (Cambridge, MA and London, 1979), ii, 338–85).

there, he must needs be restored to his former owner (*veterem ad dominum debere reverti*). For as two lawyers, Palfurius and Armillatus, have argued, every rare and beautiful thing in the wide ocean, in whatever sea it swims, belongs to the Imperial Treasury.

CHAPTER 3

The Middle Ages

GIOVANNI BOCCACCIO
1313–1375

Mr Rothfield, a Jewish moneylender, and a long-stay resident in an Edinburgh hotel – a residence associated with the promotion of his business – received a letter from the hotel management demanding that he leave the hotel effectively forthwith. Mr Rothfield, in protest, sued in the Scots courts, arguing that under Scots law an innkeeper, as in England, was obliged to receive without favour all travellers for whom accommodation was available. Lord Anderson, the lord ordinary, agreed, but when the matter was appealed to the four members of the Second Division of the Court of Session, they added an important qualification to the lord ordinary's statement of the law which entailed that Mr Rothfield had no option other than to depart. The moneylender's business transactions and where they had taken place had been the subject of adverse criticism in the press. The Second Division held, accordingly, that the standard obligation of the innkeeper was subject to a discretionary right to reject as a guest an applicant believed to be undesirable and unsuitable in view of the nature of the establishment offering accommodation and the class of guests usually accommodated there.[1]

Lord Anderson's judgment at first intance is remarkable for its history of the inn in general and in Britain in particular. At all times, Lord Anderson was to claim, in this elegant excursus, 'the leading function of the inn was to provide rest and refreshment for travellers on their journeys.' 'The writings ... of Boccaccio as to Italian ... inns make this quite clear.'[2]

GEOFFREY CHAUCER
*c.*1340–1400

In *Lawler* v. *Linden* in 1876[3] the Irish court of Common Pleas was asked to pronounce on the status within the law of master and servant of the housekeeper in a hotel in Portrush, Co. Antrim. Mr Linden, the proprietor of the Antrim

1 *Rothfield v. North British Ry. Co.*, 1920 SC 805. 2 1920 SC at 816. 3 10 ILTR 86.

Arms Hotel in the town, had in January 1876 employed Ms Lawler as housekeeper at the hotel for £40 a year. Almost at once differences arose between the parties and the plaintiff was summarily dismissed. Whether Mr Linden could have behaved in such fashion depended on the status of Ms Lawler as found by the court. If, in the contemplation of the law, she was merely a 'menial servant' – giving her an entitlement at most to a month's notice or a month's wages – then the decision of the trial jury to award her £25 was grossly excessive. The defendant sought a reduction of this award to £4 and thus raised the net issue of Ms Lawler's status.

The etymology of the adjective 'menial' dominated the argument of Denis Heron, QC, in defence of the original award, and thus in support of the contention that Ms Lawler was no 'menial' servant. Heron claimed that 'menial' was derived from 'meiny' and extended only to ordinary servants. It was so used in 'The shipmannes tale' in Chaucer's *Canterbury tales*: there the ordinary servants in the house of a shopkeeper were termed 'meiny'.[4] It was used in exactly the same sense in Shakespeare's *King Lear*.[5]

*

There is an allusion to Chaucer in Lord Anderson's elegant essay on the inn in history (see above, p. 55).

Dealing with the Middle Ages, Lord Anderson was to write, the traveller could look for necessary accommodation 'to the common inns of the country'.[6] 'These were', he continued, 'busily employed in times when the custom prevailed of making pilgrimages to holy places. The most celebrated of all pilgrimages was that described by Chaucer, where the pilgrims started from the Tabard Inn in Southwark, personally conducted by Harry Baily, the host, and put up at the "Checquers of the Hope" in Mercery Lane, Canterbury.'[7]

CERVANTES

Miguel de Cervantes Saavedra, 1547–1616

In every century, Lord Anderson was to claim, in his learned essay on the inn in history (see above, p. 55), 'the leading function of the inn was to provide rest and

4 10 ILTR at 86. 5 Act 2, scene 4. 6 *Rothfield* v. *North British Ry. Co.*, 1920 SC 805 at 816. 7 Ibid.

refreshment for travellers on their journeys.'[8] 'The writings of Le Sage and Cervantes as to Spanish inns ... make this quite clear.'[9]

MICHAEL DRAYTON
1563–1631

In the early 1890s fire broke out on no less than three separate occasions on board a ship called *The Glenlivet*. On the presentation of the predictable insurance claim, the question arose as to what precisely was meant by the word 'burnt' within the terms of the memorandum in the Lloyd's insurance policy (which was standard) – 'warranted free from average under three pounds per cent, unless general, or the ship be stranded, sunk or burnt'. In 1893, in the English Probate, Divorce and Admiralty Division, Mr Justice Gorell Barnes held that the requisite circumstances occurred when the injury by fire was sufficient to cause some interruption of the voyage, rendering the ship temporarily innavigable.[10] The Court of Appeal varied Mr Justice Gorell Barnes's conclusion, holding, rather, that the envisaged injury by fire had to constitute a substantial burning of the ship as a whole.[11] In other words, they substituted a somewhat differently worded test. Counsel for the owners of the vessel in argument before the Court of Appeal pointed out why they were unhappy with Mr Justice Gorell Barnes's judgment in the court below. 'The test adopted [there] ... that the ship must be "temporarily innavigable"', he maintained,[12]

> must also fail, because a vessel, for example, in the Irish Sea, in a strong westerly gale, might be unable to go to Dublin on account of the head wind rendering the fire unmanageable and therefore the ship innavigable, but, if turned round towards Holyhead, she might be able to navigate without difficulty whilst the fire was being got under.

At first instance, counsel for the underwriters had called in aid lines from the poet Michael Drayton's 'Battaile of Agincourt':[13]

> This ayre of France doth like me wondrous well
> Lets burne our ships, for here we mean to dwell.[14]

8 *Rothfield* v. *North British Ry. Co.*, 1920 SC 805 at 816. 9 Ibid. 10 *The Glenlivit* [1893] P. 164. 11 *The Glenlivit* [1894] P. 48. 12 [1894] P. at 50. 13 [1893] P. at 170. 14 *The works of Michael Drayton*, ed. J.W. Hebel, vol. 3 (Oxford, 1961), p. 26 ('The battaile of Agincourt', lines

without, however, insisting that 'burnt' was to be interpreted as meaning total consumption of the vessel by fire. It was a pretty literary allusion, if contributing little to the arguments being pursued and decided in the case.

The lines counsel rehearsed from Drayton's 'Battaile' are remarks attributed to Henry V on the eve of the commencement of the siege of Harfleur. They come at the conclusion of a long passage in the poem detailing the logistics of transporting so many soldiers across the English Channel. That passage had been introduced by the following stanza:

> From Milford Haven, to the mouth of Tweed,
> Ships of all burthen to Southampton brought,
> For there the King the Rendezvous decreed
> To beare aboard his most victorious fraught:
> The place from whence he with the greatest speed
> Might land in France, (of any that was thought)
> And with successe upon that lucky shore,
> Where his great Grandsire landed had before.[15]

687–8). 15 Ibid., p. 17 ('Battaile of Agincourt', lines 345–52). The entire poem boasts 2,520 lines.

CHAPTER 4

Shakespeare

HAMLET

A factor in the contested child *habeas corpus* case of *In re O'Hara*[1] was the comparative financial standing of the two households laying claim to the 11-year-old Harriet O'Hara. (For the background see below, pp. 101 and 102). In his judgment in the Irish Court of Appeal, Lord Justice Holmes solved the dilemma presented in the case, by posing a rhetorical question, the terms of which were suggested by lines in the most celebrated of the soliloquies in *Hamlet*, and furnishing one of the more obvious of answers. 'There are', Holmes argued,[2] 'dark shadows in every life. Neither the farmer's nor the peasant's child is free from trouble.' Then came the critical query and the equally critical answer:[3]

> Who will say that there is a better antidote to 'the slings and arrows of outrageous fortune'[4] than the sympathy and help that spring from family affection?

HENRY IV, PART TWO

'In the fifteenth and sixteenth centuries', writes Lord Anderson in his learned excursus on the inn in history (for the background to which see above, p. 55), a secondary function became noticeable in connexion with inns – secondary, that is, to the providing of necessary accommodation. 'They begin to be frequented for purposes of toping and conviviality.'[5] The inevitable allusion to Shakespeare follows:

> Falstaff, Poins, Doll Tearsheet, and the rest met for these purposes at 'The Boar's Head', Eastcheap.[6]

1 [1900] 2 IR 232. 2 At 256. 3 At 256–7. 4 *Hamlet*, act 3, scene 1, line 58. 5 *Rothfield v. North British Ry. Co.*, 1920 SC 805 at 816. 6 Ibid.; *Henry IV, Part Two*: see act 2, scene 4.

Lord Anderson continues the discussion:

> In Elizabeth's reign 'The Mermaid', in Bread Street, London, was a favourite haunt of Shakespeare, Jonson, Beaumont, and other poets.[7]

HENRY V

On 17 August 1940, a Major Mirrielees was killed by the accidental explosion of a hand grenade while undergoing, as a Home Guard in Perthshire in Scotland, a course of instruction by a sergeant of the regular British army.[8] That he was slain or died in the service of His Majesty was not in dispute, but the Crown was later to contend that at the time of his death he was not a 'common soldier' and thus not within the statutory provision whereby his estate would have been exempt from estate duty under the terms of the Finance Act 1894.[9] As the then lord advocate, the future Lord Reid, recalled, in a fascinating historical aperçu, the Scots parliament had long made provision for an analogous exemption.[10] Thus a statute adopted in 1513 shortly before the battle of Flodden had declared that

> gif ony man bais slaine or hurt to death in the King's armye and hoist be Englishmen or dies in the armye induring the time of his hoist his aires sall have his waird, reliefe, and mariage of the king free, dispendand with his age, quhat eild that ever be of.[11]

Whether the major could be adjudged a 'common soldier' was, as we have seen, eventually to engage the attention of the House of Lords in the case of *Blyth v. Lord Advocate*.[12] In holding that he could, the Lords reversed a decision of the Scots Court of Session.[13]

Viscount Simon found guidance on the principal issue from the passage in Henry V when the king, on the night before Agincourt, is touring the battlefield in disguise and comes upon Pistol.[14] The following conversation ensued:

> PISTOL Qui va la?
> K. HENRY A friend.

7 1920 SC at 816. **8** See *Blyth v. Lord Advocate* [1945] AC 32, at 47 *per* Lord Macmillan. **9** 57 & 58 Vict., c. 30, s. 8 (1). **10** [1945] AC at 40. **11** 1513, c. 102. **12** [1945] AC 32. **13** *Lord Advocate v. Mirrielees' Trustees*, 1943 SC 587. **14** [1945] AC at 44.

PISTOL Discuss unto me; art thou officer? Or art thou base, common, and popular?[15]

To the objection that Major Mirrielees held a rank and was therefore outwith the exempted category, Lord Macmillan had his reply ready. An Army Council instruction,[16] included by Lord Macmillan in his speech, expressly stated that the Home Guard was 'a citizen force organised on the principles of equality of service and status'. There was, accordingly, no system of 'ranks', although there were 'appointments suitably graded for the commanders of the various formations'.[17] This was later changed, but, at the time of his death, Major Mirrielees was but a company commander and held no rank as such.

HENRY VI, PART TWO

A philosophical discussion, on the part of Lord Dunedin as lord president of the Court of Session, focusing on circumstantial evidence, was prompted by a workman's compensation claim which came on appeal to the court in 1909: *Mackinnon v. Miller*.[18] Mr George Miller, the engineer on board a tug, mysteriously disappeared in the early hours of 15 February 1908. His body in night clothes was found two days later in the water close to where the tug was moored. Had he accidentally fallen from the deck or might there be a more sinister explanation? And what sort of proof had the widow under the compensation legislation to adduce? Sheriff-substitute Guy, as arbitrator, rejected outright the suggestion of suicide and, taking all the surrounding circumstances into account, held that what had befallen Mr Miller could correctly be adjudged an accident that had occurred in the course of his employment, and sufficient evidence of that had been led. The Court of Session, though invited to overturn the sheriff-substitute's conclusion, declined to do so, circumstantial evidence having been adduced to support it. The most obvious interpretation of what had transpired was buttressed by the response of the earl of Warwick to Queen Margaret's query in the *Second Part of Henry VI*: did Warwick really believe that the duke of Suffolk and Cardinal Beaufort had orchestrated the murder of the Good Duke Humphrey, the king's uncle (which, of course, they had)? It is this passage that Lord Dunedin quotes in a footnote:

15 *Henry V*, act 4, scene 1, lines 35–8. **16** No. 924 of 1940, dated 15 Aug. 1940. **17** [1945] AC at 49–50. **18** 1909 SC 373.

> Who finds the heifer dead and bleeding fresh,
> And sees fast by a butcher with an axe
> But will suspect 'twas he that made the slaughter?[19]

In the original, Shakespeare makes Warwick a trifle more expansive, but to the same effect:[20]

> Who finds the partridge in the puttock's nest,
> But may imagine how the bird was dead,
> Although the kite soar with unbloodied beak?
> Even so suspicious is this tragedy.

JULIUS CAESAR

Raised before the Irish High Court and Supreme Court in proceedings straddling 1994 and 1996 was the question of whether diminution in the pension entitlements of a judge of the District Court constituted a reduction in remuneration that could be viewed as falling foul of the Constitution.[21] The Supreme Court found that, whilst a constitutional injustice had been established, no relief was to be given the applicant district judge: rather the situation was one where the government could be relied on to introduce the necessary remedy.

Mr Justice O'Flaherty, in the course of his judgment, drew attention to the circumstance that the case itself required one group of judges to pronounce on the entitlements of a colleague, albeit one occupying a post in a lower tier of court. A word of caution was in order:[22]

> The matter calling for resolution is as follows: is the independence of the judiciary adequately secured when a judge is deprived of a sizeable share of a gratuity which he has by his contributions built up and to which it is agreed on all sides he should be entitled, except for the intervening fact of legislation which is accepted to be constitutional? I appreciate we do well when dealing with judicial colleagues to preserve a certain Caesarean detachment: *What touches us ourselves shall be last serv'd* (Shakespeare: *Julius Caesar*, Act III, Sc. 1).[23] Nonetheless, judges of the District Court are entitled to the same measure of justice as anyone else in the land who appears in this Court: no more and no less …

19 *Second Part of Henry VI*, act 3, scene 2, lines 188–90. **20** Ibid., lines 191–4. **21** *District Judge McMenamin v. Ireland* [1996] 3 IR 100. **22** [1996] 3 IR at 143. **23** Line 8.

The words from *Julius Caesar* quoted here by Mr Justice O'Flaherty are spoken by Caesar himself. There is irony in the choice of the occasion and in the choice of the language. Artemidorus urged Caesar now on his way to the Forum on the Ides of March to give priority to a communication of his in preference to a second communication presented by Decius. Caesar declined: 'What touches us ourselves shall be last serv'd.' The rest, as they say, is history.

KING LEAR

'Be Kent unmannerly, When Lear is mad.' With these words in the very first dramatic scene in *King Lear*,[24] the earl of Kent defends his intervention to protest at Lear's dividing of his kingdom between Goneril and Regan and the disinheriting of his youngest daughter, Cordelia. 'Reverse thy doom', Kent continues:[25]

> And in thy best consideration check
> This hideous rashness …
> Thy youngest daughter does not love thee least;
> Nor are those empty-hearted whose low sound
> Reverbs no hollowness.

Lear is furious, and the upshot is that he imposes a sentence of banishment on Kent.[26] It was not a wise move.

The identical seven words formed the peroration of a speech by Isaac Butt, QC in defence of an attorney, one James Barry, in proceedings before the Irish court of Common Pleas in April 1869.[27] On 14 April that year the *Cork Examiner* contained a report of a speech made by Barry at a public meeting criticising the court that had recently unseated a successful parliamentary candidate.[28] Summoned to appear before the court to explain his remarks, Barry protested that the report had not been accurate. At this, Mr Justice Keogh ordered Barry to state on affidavit to be produced in court what portion of the newspaper report he admitted to be correct and what portion he considered to be wrong. The notion that an attorney could be forced in this fashion himself to furnish the evidence which might make him liable to attachment for contempt infuriated members of the profession, and the point was uppermost in Butt's mind when on 27 April he appeared on Barry's behalf before the court of

24 Act 1, scene 1, lines 147–8. **25** Ibid., lines 151–6. **26** Ibid., lines 169–82. **27** *Youghal Election Petition (Barry's Case)* (1869) IR 3 CL 537. **28** Reported as the *Youghal Election Petition* (1869) IR 3 CL 530.

Common Pleas. On the occasion Butt did not mince words. The speech caused a sensation (and was to be fully reported in the law reports)[29] and had the desired effect, Mr Justice Keogh's order concerning the affidavit being discharged.[30] The peroration included this unusual language:[31]

> I know that the truest reverence for authority is often manifested by boldly remonstrating when it is going wrong –
>
> Be Kent unmannerly
> When Lear is mad.

*

In *Lawler v. Linden* in 1876[32] the Irish court of Common Pleas was asked to pronounce on the status within the then law of master and servant of the housekeeper in a hotel in Portrush, Co. Antrim. Mr Linden, the proprietor of the Antrim Arms Hotel in the town had in January 1876, as we have previously recalled (see above, p. 55), employed Ms Lawler as housekeeper at the hotel for £40 a year. Almost at once differences were to arise between the parties, and the plaintiff was summarily dismissed. Whether Mr Linden could have behaved in such fashion depended on the status of Ms Lawler as found by the court. If, in the contemplation of the law, she was merely a 'menial servant' – giving her an entitlement at most to a month's notice or a month's wages – then the decision of the trial jury to award her £25 was grossly excessive. The defendant sought a reduction of this award to £4 and thus raised the net issue of Ms Lawler's status.

The etymology of the adjective 'menial' dominated the argument of Denis Heron, QC, in defence of the original award, and thus in support of the contention that Ms Lawler was no 'menial' servant. Heron claimed that 'menial' was derived from 'meiny' and extended only to ordinary servants. It was so used in *King Lear* where in act 2, scene 4, Kent whom Regan and Cornwall had placed in the stocks, informs Lear of their sudden departure, following news from Goneril: 'They summon'd up their meiny, straight took horse'.[33] It was used in the same sense in Chaucer.[34] 'A housekeeper in a great hotel', Heron insisted, 'has charge of the linen, the china, and the still-room; she is not a menial servant.'[35] The court of Common Pleas agreed. 'Circumstances change

29 Ibid., at 541–9; E.A. Plunkett, 'Attorneys and solicitors in Ireland' in *Record of the centenary of the charter of the Incorporated Law Society of Ireland, 1852–1952* (Dublin, 1953), 38 at 60. **30** Judgment of the full court, delivered by Chief Justice Monahan: IR 3 CL 549–51. **31** IR 3 CL at 548. **32** 10 ILTR 86. **33** *King Lear*, act 2, scene 4, line 35; 10 ILTR at 86. **34** Ibid. **35** Ibid.

in the progress of civilisation', Chief Justice Morris observed, 'and the question now arises, is the housekeeper of a large hotel a menial or domestic servant?'[36] He thought not, and explained why:

> In a large hotel the housekeeper is in a most responsible position, as a kind of manageress; in fact, in some large hotels owned by a limited company, she must actually be the manageress of the entire establishment.[37]

MACBETH

John Toler, later to be ennobled as Lord Norbury and made chief justice of the Irish Common Pleas, prosecuted Henry and James Sheares for treason at the Dublin special commission in July 1798.[38] He spiced his introductory remarks with a number of literary quotations.[39] Prominent among these were lines taken from *Macbeth*, designed to impress upon the jury the serious nature of a proclamation that had been found among the brothers Sheares' possessions – damning evidence indeed. There was not a single line in it, Toler expostulated, which was but to teach 'Bloody instructions, which being taught return to plague the inventor'[40] – sentiments expressed by Macbeth as he contemplated the murder of King Duncan: 'If it were done when 'tis done, then 'twere well / it were done quickly.'[41]

*

A century later Mr Justice O'Brien was to employ a further short passage from this speech of Macbeth's pondering Duncan's fate, when charging the jury at the conclusion of a sensational trial at the Clonmel assizes.[42] Here, in July 1895, Michael Cleary and others were to stand trial for the death of Bridget, his wife. Placed over an open fire – ostensibly to secure the release from her human frame of an evil spirit who had entered into possession of that entire frame – Bridget, not altogether surprisingly, had burnt to death. The gravity of what had occurred was not concealed by the trial judge when he came to charge the jury:

> A young woman in the opening of her life was put to death – a young married woman, who, suspecting no harm, guilty of no offence, virtuous

36 10 ILTR at 87. **37** Ibid. **38** *R. v. Henry and John Sheares*, 27 Howell St. Tr. 296. **39** Ibid., at 296–7. **40** *Macbeth*, act 1, scene 7, lines 8–10. **41** Ibid., lines 1–2. **42** *R. v. Cleary, Irish Times*, 5 July 1895.

and respectable in all her conduct and all her proceedings – from those of all others who were bound to protect her, from the hands of her own husband, who swore at the altar to cherish and protect her, and from her own father, has met her death under circumstances which remind me of the lines:

> Pleading like angels trumpet-tongued against
> The deep damnation of her taking-off.[43]

MEASURE FOR MEASURE

A Mr Callingham who lived in Buckinghamshire at Beaconsfield was the owner of a garden of high standard to which he admitted the public, making a charge for charitable purposes. In the 1920s he acquired adjoining land and in 1928 work was begun there to create a model village. Within the village itself a variety of buildings was to be constructed: a church, schools, a post office – an interesting inclusion in view of contemporary concerns over the fate of such offices in rural England – and council offices. There was also to be a model railway on the site. So far as the buildings were concerned, these were from two to four feet high on the scale of one inch to a foot. Most were constructed of stone or brick and fixed to concrete bases on the ground. Partially completed by 1931, the village that year was regularly opened to the public. The village had come to be designated the Bekonscot Model Village.[44]

In 1950 the county council, as the local planning authority, issued an enforcement notice under legislation of 1947,[45] requiring the demolition or removal of the village, insisting that developments on the site contravened previous planning controls.[46]

Part of the village had been completed prior to 1 October 1929 when the local authority had passed a resolution that had the effect, the local authority contended, of obliging landowners planning development in the local authority's area thereafter to seek permission. Mr Callingham's advisors in the proceedings taken by him to have the enforcement notice set aside, were also to argue that

43 *Macbeth*, act 1, scene 7, lines 19–20. Mr Justice O'Brien, makes two changes from the original text: 'pleading' for 'will plead' and 'her' for 'his' [i.e. King Duncan's]. See further Angela Bourke, *The burning of Bridget Cleary* (London, 1999). 44 These facts are drawn from the rehearsal of them to be found in the report of the resultant law-suit; see below. 45 Town and Country Planning Act 1947 (10 & 11 Geo. VI, c. 51). 46 Introduced by the resolution, referred to below, authorised by the Town Planning (General Interim Development) Order, 1922.

the miniature buildings on the site did not constitute 'buildings' for purposes of a section in relevant legislation of 1932.[47]

Justices ruled in favour of Mr Callingham but, first, the Divisional Court and, later, the Court of Appeal quashed that determination, holding that the key section in the act of 1947 applied to all the model houses and other things put up since 1 October 1929 and that because these had been erected in contravention of planning controls in place before the act of 1947 came into force, the enforcement notice issued by Buckinghamshire County Council was valid.[48]

The consequence that part of the model village might remain but the rest demolished proved of some concern to one member of the Court of Appeal, Mr Justice Lloyd-Jacob. 'The mutilation of the present layout', he observed,[49]

> by destruction of the remainder would appear to serve no useful purpose to anyone. This, however cogent for consideration by the Minister, is not a matter which concerns the court.

A second member of the Court of Appeal, Lord Justice Morris, whilst concurring with his colleagues, found the conduct of the local authority in the affair somewhat strange, albeit deciding in the end to give them the benefit of the doubt, and quoting from *Measure for Measure* in the process. 'It may seem somewhat incongruous', Lord Justice Morris began,[50]

> that the county council should abandon complaint in regard to user of land for the purpose of a public exhibition known as Bekonscot Model Village, but should still proceed with a demand for the demolition or removal of some of the buildings which have for years been publicly exhibited as and have become known as Bekonscot Model Village.
>
> It is found by the justices that since as long ago as August, 1929, members of the public have been admitted to the area, and that by April 1, 1933, the model village was substantially completed.

'But', he continued,[51] signifying a change of gear that did not bode well for Mr Callingham (and making use of remarks uttered by Isabella in one of her altercations with Angelo in *Measure for Measure*),[52]

47 Mr H. Willis, arguendo, [1952] 2 QB at 521. **48** *Buckingham County Council v. Callingham* [1952] 2 QB 515. **49** [1952] 2 QB at 533. **50** [1952] 2 QB at 529. **51** [1952] 2 QB at 529–30. **52** *Measure for Measure*, act 2, scene 2, line 107.

> the task of the court can only be to decide whether the county council has been endowed with 'a giant's strength'; the court has not the material before it to decide whether 'it is tyrannous to use it like a giant.'

In 1923, in proceedings before the King's Bench Division, Mr Justice Coleridge had incorporated the same lines from *Measure for Measure* in a judgment in which he stigmatised the conduct of the National Union of Foundry Workers of Great Britain and Ireland for their refusal to reinstate one of its members, one Samuel Blackall, for supposed non-compliance with a rule on the payment of union dues.[53] It was difficult, Mr Justice Coleridge argued,[54] to be restrained about the conduct of the shop steward and of the branch committee which had been brought to his attention:

> O! it is excellent
> To have a giant's strength; but it is tyrannous
> To use it like a giant.

This passage from *Measure for Measure*, cited in two very different contexts in the *Callingham* and *Blackall* cases, follows on from Isabella's original intercession with the corrupt judge, Angelo, to pardon her brother Claudio for his offence of fornication. The odds are against her succeeding. Angelo had earlier proclaimed:[55]

> We must not make a scarecrow of the law,
> Setting it up to fear the birds of prey,
> And let it keep one shape, till custom make it
> Their perch, and not their terror.

Isabella nevertheless pressed Angelo to show pity, to which he retorts that he shows that most of all when he shows 'justice'.[56] 'Your brother dies to-morrow', Angelo insists; 'be content'.[57] At this Isabella rebels, alluding to the strength of a giant and that it was tyrannical even so to deploy such strength. More follows from her in an extraordinarily powerful attack:[58]

> Could great men thunder
> As Jove himself does, Jove would ne'er be quiet,

53 *Blackall v. National Union of Foundry Workers of Great Britain and Ireland* (1923) 39 Times LR 431. 54 39 Times LR at 432. 55 *Measure for Measure*, act 2, scene 1, lines 1–4. 56 Act 2, scene 2, line 100. 57 Ibid., line 105. 58 Ibid., lines 110–23.

> For every pelting, petty officer
> Would use his heaven for thunder.
> Nothing but thunder! Merciful Heaven,
> Thou rather with thy sharp and sulphurous bolt
> Split'st the unwedgeable and gnarled oak
> Than the soft myrtle: but man, proud man,
> Drest in a little brief authority,
> Most ignorant of what he's most assured,
> His glassy essence, like an angry ape,
> Plays such fantastic tricks before high heaven
> As make the angels weep; who with our spleens,
> Would all themselves laugh mortal.

Many angels, of course, continue to weep.

MERCHANT OF VENICE

Boyle v. Lee and Goyns in 1991[59] witnessed another attempt by the Irish Supreme Court to clarify the solution to problems in Irish conveyancing, generated by the requirement introduced by the Statute of Frauds in 1695,[60] that there must always exist a sufficient note or memorandum of the agreement buttressing any actual transaction. In the circumstances of the case, the decision that prevailed was to the effect that the essential terms of the envisaged contract had not been finalised and that therefore there was no compliance with the requirements of the Statute of Frauds.

Where writing produced as evidence of the requisite note or memorandum yet stated that the whole agreement was 'subject to contract', legal precedent examined by Mr Justice McCarthy in the case seemed, on his view of the case-law, not to be entirely consistent or straightforward.[61] Where the words 'subject to contract' were a feature, the correct approach, in his estimation, was to hold that the rule sanctioned by the Statute of Frauds had not been complied with. The tone of the judge's remarks becomes markedly philosophical as he continues, even introducing a tag from Shakespeare. 'It may well be thought', the judge adds,

> that this rigidity of construction will result in genuine bargains not being enforced and that a court should, as I believe it has in the past, 'to do a great

59 [1992] ILRM 65. **60** 7 Will. III, c. 7, s. 2. **61** [1992] ILRM at 80.

right, do a little wrong' (see *Merchant of Venice*, act 4, scene 1, l. 215). It is reasonable to assume that the writing requirement is well known to owners and buyers of land; Portia's rule of construction is the preferred alternative.[62]

*

A longer quotation from the same scene in *The Merchant of Venice* was incorporated into his judgment by Lord Justice Russell in *Sydall v. Castings Ltd.* in 1966.[63] The net issue here was whether an illegitimate child was eligible for benefit in a group life assurance scheme as a 'descendant' of one of the assured. The child in question was one Yvette Lorraine Sydall. The county court judge held that Yvette was eligible and in the Court of Appeal, Lord Denning, the master of the rolls, agreed. But Lord Denning's two colleagues, Lord Justice Diplock and Lord Justice Russell, did not. The word 'descendant' in a legal document had to be construed, they argued, as a term of art, and so construed, its meaning indicated blood relationship in the legitimate line. Lord Justice Russell was to take some pains to distance himself from the approach of Lord Denning. 'I may perhaps be forgiven', he concludes his judgment,[64]

> for saying that it appears to me that Lord Denning M.R. has acceded to the appeal of Bassanio in the *Merchant of Venice*.
>
> > *Bassanio*: 'And, I beseech you,
> > Wrest once the law to your authority:
> > To do a great right, do a little wrong'.[65]
>
> But Portia retorted:[66]
>
> > *Portia*: 'It must not be: there is no power in Venice
> > Can alter a decree established:
> > 'Twill be recorded for a precedent,
> > And many an error, by the same example,
> > Will rush into the State: it cannot be.'
>
> I am a Portia man.

62 Ibid. **63** [1967] 1 QB 302. **64** [1967] 1 QB at 321–2. **65** *Merchant of Venice*, act 4, scene 1, lines 213–15. **66** Ibid., lines 216–20.

*

At the Bristol Crown Court, in 1993, one Stephen Cooke was convicted of offences of rape and kidnapping for which he received sentences of ten years and two years respectively. DNA evidence showed a correlation between a hair sample taken from Cooke and semen in the victim's vagina and a camisole. At the trial before Mr Justice Mantell, objection was taken to the admission of this evidence on the grounds that the hair sample had been wrongfully obtained, it consisting not just of hair itself but also of the sheath at the root of the hair. The trial judge disallowed the objection, and that ruling was later upheld by the Court of Appeal (Lord Justice Glidewell, Mr Justice Blofeld and Mr Justice Buxton) who dismissed the appeal. For Mr Justice Mantell the argument that the hair and the sheath could be distinguished brought to mind the contention advanced by Portia addressing Shylock in *The Merchant of Venice*: 'Take thou thy pound of flesh ... but [not] one drop of Christian blood.' But the argument did not win him over. Lord Justice Glidewell, in his judgment for the Court of Appeal,[67] repeated at the relevant stage in his reasoning this allusion to Shakespeare. Portia's critical intervention in *Shylock v. Antonio* merits being set out at length. 'This bond', she insisted,[68]

> doth give thee here no jot of blood;
> The words expressly are 'a pound of flesh':
> Take then thy bond, take thou thy pound of flesh;
> But, in the cutting it, if thou dost shed
> One drop of Christian blood, thy lands and goods
> Are, by the laws of Venice, confiscate
> Unto the state of Venice.

*

Under section 5 of the Government of Ireland Act, as originally enacted[69] – it was to be subsequently modified – the Parliament of Northern Ireland was debarred from making any law so as either directly or indirectly to take any property without compensation. The compulsory acquisition by the Northern Ireland Road Transport Board, under legislation passed in 1935,[70] of all existing road motor undertakings operated for hire or reward was queried in litigation in

67 *R. v. Stephen Cooke* (1995) 1 Cr. App. Rep. 318; *Daily Telegraph*, 18 January 2006. **68** *Merchant of Venice*, act 4, scene 1, lines 306–12. **69** 10 & 11 Geo. V, c. 67. **70** Road and Railway Transport Act (N.I.) 1935 (25 & 26 Geo. V, c. 15).

1940 in the case of an undertaking that commenced operations after June 1934, on the grounds that, in the particular circumstances, section 5 had been breached and that the legislation concerned was *pro tanto* unconstitutional: *N.I.R.T.B. v. Benson*.[71] Benson had been allowed to continue his operations after the Act of 1935 came into force, but the consent to do so was withdrawn in 1937. The disallowance of any compensation in respect of Benson's loss of goodwill was at the centre of the constitutional challenge.[72] A majority of the Court of Appeal held that this was no 'taking', and the legislation was accordingly valid. Lord Justice Babington dissented, and in his lengthy examination of the meaning of the word 'take'[73] employs an illustration from the *Merchant of Venice*. 'Standing by itself', he writes,[74]

> the word [take] is ambiguous and unless it be used with a qualifying adverb or in conjunction with some object, it is impossible to give it a precise meaning. For example, it may mean 'take over' suggesting a transfer of possession, or it may mean 'take away' signifying to dispossess or confiscate, or it may connote mere destruction as when the highwayman says 'Your money or your life', meaning 'Give me your money or I will take your life'. Shakespeare uses the word in all these senses when Shylock says
>
> You take my house, when you do take the prop
> That doth maintain my house; you take my life,
> When you do take the means whereby I live.[75]

A MIDSUMMER NIGHT'S DREAM

The playlet 'Pyramus and Thisbe' performed by Quince, Bottom and the others in act 5 of *A midsummer night's dream* was aptly recalled by Baron Dowse of the Irish court of Exchequer in 1876 in the curious affair of *Dolan v. Kavanagh*.[76] Kavanagh was a provision merchant in occupation of premises at 30 Talbot Street, Dublin. He was proceeded against for exposing bacon, ham, ling and cheese for sale outside his shop, contrary to the provisions of a statute of 5 Victoria.[77] Kavanagh's defence was that the goods in question were not displayed outside his shop, though on view in the open air, arguing that the

71 [1940] N.I. 133. 72 The prosecution at petty sessions had been dismissed. On an appeal to quarter sessions, the deputy recorder of Belfast had stated a case for the opinion of the higher court. 73 [1940] N.I. at 156–61. 74 [1940] N.I. at 157. 75 *Merchant of Venice*, act 4, scene 1, lines 375–7. 76 (1876) IR 10 CL 166. 77 5 Vict., sess. 2, c. 24, s. 17(7).

raised pavement, formerly surrounded by railings, in front of no. 30, upon which the goods were indeed displayed constituted part of the premises and thus part of the shop. Baron Dowse, adopting a commonsensical view of the matter, was not impressed. 'I decline', he wrote,[78] 'to construct a non-existent wall [Kavanagh's contention] and to construe an Act of Parliament by giving to "airy nothings a local habitation and a name".'[79]

More was to come, continuing the mention of Shakespeare:[80]

> When 'Snout the tinker', represented a wall [in 'Pyramus and Thisbe'], he brought with him some roughcast and stone; we are to be more fantastic than the 'Midsummer night's dream', and to build a wall without even the smallest thread of gossamer to assist us. If we build the wall, how long is it to endure? Till this case is over; and then, in this, at least, resembling the wall of the poet, it will say:-
>
> 'Thus have I, wall, my part discharged so;
> And being done, this wall away doth go.'[81]

'I will be no party', the judge continued, 'to this castle building in the air. If the person convicted here wants an unsubstantial wall, let him have unsubstantial hams and bacons exposed for sale.'

*

'Pyramus and Thisbe' was to be recalled in different proceedings over sixty years later. In *Lambert v. F. W. Woolworth and Co.* in 1938[82] the Court of Appeal (Lord Justices Greer, Slesser and MacKinnon) were faced with the problem of interpretation of the word 'improvement' in the English Landlord and Tenant Act, 1927.[83] Where a covenant in a lease forbade the making of improvements by the tenant without the consent of the landlord, such consent could not be unreasonably withheld. In the circumstances of the case, a majority (Lord Justices Slesser and MacKinnon) held that what the tenant, Woolworths, were planning for commercial premises occupied by them in Bournemouth constituted an 'improvement' and that the landlord, Lamberts, had unreasonably withheld their consent. The action had been commenced by the latter, seeking a declaration to the effect that Woolworths' planned alterations did not constitute an improve-

78 IR 10 CL at 172. **79** The words are those of Theseus: *A midsummer night's dream*, act 5, scene 1, lines 16–17. **80** IR 10 CL at 172. **81** *A midsummer night's dream*, act 5, scene 1, lines 207–8. **82** [1938] Ch. 883. **83** 17 & 18 Geo. V, c. 36, s. 19 (2).

ment. In earlier proceedings in the same affair that had also arrived before a differently constituted Court of Appeal,[84] one of the judges, Lord Justice Greene, had adopted a strict approach to the interpretation of the word 'improvement'. That approach evoked no sympathy from the majority of the court in the 1938 appeal. The making of an opening, as of a door, in the demised premises impressed Lord Justice Slesser as 'no more and no less an improvement than the removal of the wall' (which was the principal feature of the proposed alterations).[85] If it was objectionable, as Lord Justice Greene appeared to have held, to consider the effect upon the premises being joined, as per Woolworths' plans, in considering the case of the wall, so also it had to be in the case of a door.

Lines from *A midsummer night's dream* were then, appropriately enough, brought into the reckoning. 'A wall', continued Lord Justice Slesser,[86] 'may be a detriment, its removal an improvement:

> 'O wall', Thisbe laments, 'full often hast thou heard my moans, For parting my fair Pyramus and me!'[87]

MUCH ADO ABOUT NOTHING

In May 1835 Archdeacon Knox, rector of the parish of Aglish in Co. Tipperary, began a suit for non-payment of tithe against one Gavan, a local defaulter. These proceedings were commenced in the Irish court of Exchequer and, with Gavan studiously ignoring them, Knox sued out a writ of rebellion. Under this procedure commissioners were designated to apprehend Gavan and bring him forcibly before the Exchequer in Dublin by a stipulated date. Dudley, one of the commissioners, sought the assistance of the police stationed in Borrisokane close to Gavan's place of abode. The chief constable there, one Malone, referred the request for assistance to the then head of the Munster provincial constabulary, a Major Miller. Miller in turn passed on the request to Dublin Castle. From there Miller was told that he 'might decline compliance'. Dublin Castle, in short, was not prepared to assist in the due enforcement of civil legal process.[88]

The barons of the Exchequer took a jaundiced view of the actions – rather the

84 *Woolworths (F.W) & Co. Ltd. v. Lambert* [1937] Ch. 37. **85** [1938] Ch. at 903. **86** Ibid. **87** *A midsummer night's dream*, act 5, scene 1, lines 190–1. **88** For a recital of these facts, see *Knox v. Gavan* (1836) 1 Jones 190; and see further W.N. Osborough, 'Executive failure to enforce judicial decrees: a neglected chapter in nineteenth-century constitutional history' in John McEldowney and Paul O'Higgins (eds), *The common law tradition: essays in Irish legal history* (Dublin, 1990), pp 85–116.

inaction – of the executive. Baron Smith made his views abundantly clear. 'The title of the King's constitutionally established writs', he wrote,[89]

> to unstinted and full obedience, I consider to be part of the law of the land; and to be so (by the way) for the benefit of the people, and in advancement of their rights. I consequently hold, that the executive can have no right to stint or curtail or shackle an obedience, which is due and owing, by the law of the land.

Earlier in his judgment, the baron had gone to considerable lengths to castigate the behaviour of the police.[90] That behaviour called to mind, Smith lamented, Dogberry's charge to the watch in *Much ado about nothing*,[91] which, it hardly needed saying, embraced no acceptable principle of sound policy:

DOGBERRY	This is your charge: you shall comprehend all vagrom men; you are to bide any man stand, in the prince's name.
2ND WATCHMAN	How if a' will not stand?
DOGBERRY	Why, then, take no note of him, but let him go; and presently call the rest of the watch together, and thank God you are rid of a Knave. ... If you meet a thief, you may suspect him, by virtue of your office, to be no true man; and, for such kind of men, the less you meddle or make with them, why, the more is for your honesty.
WATCHMAN	If we know him to be a thief, shall we not lay hands on him?
DOGBERRY	Truly, by your office you may; but I think they that touch pitch will be defiled: the most peaceable way for you, if you do take a thief, is to let him show himself what he is, and steal out of your company.

OTHELLO

In *Nisbet v. Rayne & Burn* in 1910[92] the English Court of Appeal dismissed an appeal against an award of £300 to the plaintiff under workmen's compensation

89 1 Jones at 236–37. **90** 1 Jones at 229–30. **91** Act 3, scene 3, lines 25–31, 53–63. **92** [1910] 2 KB 689.

legislation in respect of the death of her husband. He had been murdered at Morpeth in the north of England when travelling by train with a large sum of money for paying his employer's workmen. The validity of the award made in Mrs Nisbet's favour depended on the answer to the question whether her husband's murder could properly be described as an accident arising out of and in the course of his employment. The Court of Appeal held that it could but, in the process, members of the court conceded the difficulty that in ordinary parlance deliberate killings were not customarily treated as accidents. Lord Justice Kennedy took as an example an incident in Scots history. 'An historian', he argued, 'who described the end of Rizzio by saying that he met with a fatal accident in Holyrood Palace would fairly, I suppose, be charged with a misleading statement of fact.'[93] Lord Justice Farwell admitted as much too, basing his argument on the circumstances of Desdemona's death at the hands of Othello.

> Although it is true that one would not in ordinary parlance say, for example, that Desdemona died by accident, this is because the horror of the crime dominates the imagination and compels the expression of the situation in terms relating to the crime and the criminal alone.[94]

Lord Justice Kennedy, for his part, sought to escape the consequences for Mrs Nisbet of his interpretation of the killing of Rizzio by introducing further considerations that merited being weighed in the balance – not that the stratagem, as we will soon discover, earned the unanimous approval of the House of Lords in a later case. 'Whilst the description of death by murderous violence as an "accident"', the judge continued,

> cannot honestly be said to accord with the common understanding of the word, wherein is implied a negation of wilfulness and intention, I conceive it to be my duty rather to stretch the meaning of the word from the narrower to the wider sense of which it is inherently and etymologically capable, that is 'any unforeseen and untoward event producing a personal harm', than to exclude from the operation of this section a class of injury which it is quite unreasonable to suppose that the Legislature did not intend to include within it.[95]

The clubbing to death of a seemingly unpopular assistant master at an industrial school in Trim, Co. Meath, in 1912 by pupils at the school raised the

93 Ibid., at 696. 94 Ibid., at 693–4. 95 Ibid., at 696.

identical problem of interpretation under the Workmen's Compensation Act 1906.[96] Mrs Kelly was awarded £100 compensation in respect of the death of her son, the assistant master. The Irish Court of Appeal confirmed that award, as did the House of Lords, but the latter only on a split vote of 4–3.[97] Among the minority that sought to overturn the award in favour of Mrs Kelly, Lord Dunedin took issue with the approach that had found favour with Lord Justice Kennedy in *Nisbet v. Rayne & Burn*. 'I can scarcely conceive a proceeding more illegitimate', he declared.[98] For the majority, Lord Shaw of Dunfermline, on the other hand, introduced an argument that had not been rehearsed in so stark a fashion in *Nisbet's* case. 'It is surely part of ... popular and ordinary signification', he was to assert, 'that for seventy years in England the word "accident" has been publicly and descriptively used as inclusive of occurrences intentionally caused.'[99]

Both Lord Dunedin, for the minority, and Lord Shaw of Dunfermline, for the majority, revisit the deaths of Rizzio and Desdemona and the vexed matter of how best to describe them from a restricted vocabulary.[1] Lord Shaw appeared poised not to offer any fresh view when he remarked that he did not intend to carry the controversy over usage of the word 'accident' into what he termed 'the wider literary field', since he considered that 'in that field the interest is apt to exceed the relevancy'.[2] But, in the event, it was this member of the House of Lords who, more than any other member of the majority, was to deduce most from *Othello* and, in so doing, to nail his colours very firmly to the mast, and thus to ensure for Mrs Kelly the decisive vote in her favour. 'Judges', Lord Shaw began,[3]

> have girded at Farwell L.J.'s instance of Desdemona's murder, and I do not disagree with them. But I should have thought, on the other hand, that when a certain 'unvarnished tale' was delivered 'of moving accidents by flood and field', the term put into the mouth of Othello was hardly meant to be exclusive of the perils of wilful onset, of seizure by 'the insolent foe', or of any other intended and 'distressful stroke'.[4]

*

96 6 Edw. VII, c. 58. **97** *Trim Joint District School Board of Management v. Kelly* [1914] AC 667. **98** Ibid., at 689. **99** Ibid., at 708. **1** Rizzio's death and Desdemona's are revisited by Lord Dunedin: [1914] AC at 689. **2** [1914] AC at 708. **3** Ibid. **4** These quotations are taken from an earlier scene in *Othello*: act 1, scene 3, lines 90, 135, 137, 157 – the scene where Othello describes to the duke of Venice highlights of his eventful career.

Othello was revisited by the House of Lords in the hearing of the criminal appeal in *Holmes v. D.P.P.* in 1946.[5] Advancing doctrine that today would certainly be regarded as questionable, the Lords held that a confession of adultery by a wife could not ground a defence of provocation for the husband, leading to a verdict of manslaughter rather than one of murder. In a robust rejection of any such change in the law, Viscount Simon also dealt with the variant case where intelligence of adultery was communicated to the spouse affected by a third party. It was Desdemona's fate to which Simon was to refer. 'Even if Iago's insinuations against Desdemona's virtue had been true', he remarked, 'Othello's crime was murder and nothing else.'[6]

RICHARD II

Although the Irish Free State Constitution of 1922 was to be superseded by the new Irish Constitution of 1937 (which is still in force), the protracted discussion in both the High Court and the Supreme Court of the amendment power associated with the former Constitution remains of considerable interest. The discussion occurs in *The State (Ryan) v. Lennon*[7] where the High Court and the Supreme Court (but only by a 2–1 majority in the latter court) upheld the validity of changes made to the 1922 Constitution, changes made by ordinary legislation but outside the initial eight-year period when, according to Article 50 of the Constitution, changes could be effectuated in this more informal fashion. An amendment passed by ordinary legislation allowing for adoption of future amendments by the informal procedure of ordinary legislation for 16 years as opposed to 8 thus passed muster – but plainly to the dismay of Chief Justice Kennedy, the dissenter in the Supreme Court.

Controversy centred on the Constitution (Amendment No. 17) Act, 1931, which introduced a new article, Article 2A, into the 1922 Constitution, which provided for a Special Powers Tribunal to try certain kinds of case.

In a curious peroration in his judgment in the Supreme Court – the precise significance of which it must be left to each reader to decide for him or herself – Mr Justice FitzGibbon was to find space for a quotation from John of Gaunt's dying speech in *Richard II*, delivered just before the arrival on to the stage of the king, and thus delivered in his absence.[8]

'It can never again be suggested', Mr Justice FitzGibbon writes,

5 [1946] AC 588. 6 [1946] AC at 598. 7 [1935] IR 170. 8 [1935] IR at 236–7.

that the Saorstát has obtained citizens by false pretences, now that the Oireachtas has promulgated *urbi et orbi*, to the Czechoslovak and the Mexican, to our kinsmen in the United States of America and throughout the British Commonwealth of Nations, and, above all, to our fellow-countrymen in Northern Ireland, whose co-operation we profess to desire, as well as to all those who seek, or acquire, or have thrust upon them, rights under our new Irish Nationality and Citizenship Act, Amendment No. 17 as an integral part of our Constitution, setting forth in the clearest language, in the forefront of that document, the conditions under which liberty is enjoyed and justice may be administered in

> This other Eden, demi-paradise,
> ...
> This precious stone set in the silver sea,
> ...
> This blessed plot, this earth, this realm, this [Saor Stát].[9]

RICHARD III

There is much that is quotable in the concluding address at the trial of major war criminals at Nuremberg of Mr Justice Jackson, leading prosecution counsel. An apt quotation from *Richard III*, for instance, was to feature in the peroration.[10]

The defendants brazenly uttered false statements and resorted to double talk. There were also, Mr Justice Jackson claimed, 'other circumventions of truth in the nature of fantastic explanations and absurd professions.' Unsurprisingly, [c]redibility [had become] one of the main issues of this Trial.'

'It is against such a background', Prosecutor Jackson avers,

> that these defendants now ask this Tribunal to say that they are not guilty of planning, executing, or conspiring to commit this long list of crimes and wrongs. They stand before the record of this Trial as bloodstained Gloucester stood by the body of his slain King. He begged of the widow, as they beg of you: 'Say I slew them not'. And the Queen replied, 'Then say they were not slain. But dead they are ...'.[11] If you were to say of these men

9 *Richard II*, act 2, scene 1, lines 42, 46, 50. 10 *Trial of the major war criminals*, vol. 19 (1948), pp 431 ff. 11 *Richard III*, act 1, scene 2, lines 82–90.

> that they are not guilty, it would be as true to say that there has been no war, there are no slain, there has been no crime.[12]

*

The 'defence' of superior orders, also brought up in Nuremberg, it is worth recording, was to be disallowed in the case of an associate of the regicides placed on trial after the restoration of Charles II in 1660. Lord Chief Justice Kelyng (? 1607–1671) related the circumstances:[13]

> Memorandum, that upon the trial of one Axtell, a soldier, who commanded the guards at the king's trial, and at his murder; he justified that all he did was as a soldier, by the command of his superior officer, whom he must obey or die. It was resolved that was no excuse, for his superior was a traitor, and all that joined him in that *act* were traitors and did by that approve the treason; and where the command is traitorous, there the obedience to that command is also traitorous.

TWELFTH NIGHT

Adoption by Westminster City Council of a controversial policy to sell council houses to sitting tenants with a view to boost the chances of electoral success for the Conservative Party generated in the late 1990s litigation that principally concerned the council's leader, Dame Shirley Porter, and deputy leader, Mr David Weeks.[14] Opposition councillors objected that, in the circumstances, the policy and its implementations were unlawful, and seized the local government auditor of their concerns. The latter agreed that the policy was unlawful, and proceeded to issue his certificate to the effect that substantial losses had been occasioned to the council through 'wilful misconduct', chargeable against the individuals deemed answerable. The Divisional Court dismissed appeals by Porter and Weeks, but this decision was overturned by the Court of Appeal. The House of Lords, however, unanimously reversed the Court of Appeal.[15] Lord

12 Jackson attributes the reply to Queen Margaret; this is a mistake. The utterance comes from the Lady Anne, later Richard III's wife, who was the widow of the Prince of Wales, Henry VI's son. 13 Kelyng 13, 84 ER 1060. See further *Oxford DNB*, s.v. Axtell, Daniel (?1622–1660). Col. Axtell had had military experience in Ireland, where he had been court-martialled for killing prisoners taken near Banagher, Co. Offaly, after promise of quarter. 14 On management of affairs on Westminster City Council during the period, see Andrew Hosken, *Nothing like a dame: the scandals of Shirley Porter* (London, 2006), reviewed by Jenny Diski, *London Review of Books*, 25 May 2006, p. 13. 15 *Porter v. Magill* [2002] 2 AC 357.

Scott of Foscote seized the bull by the horns, when, in the opening paragraph of his concurring speech, he used language that could not have been more bluntly expressed and found space for a Shakespearean allusion.[16] 'My Lords', he began,

> this is a case about political corruption. The corruption was not money corruption. No one took a bribe. No one sought or received money for political favours. But there are other forms of corruption, often less easily detectable and therefore more insidious. Gerrymandering, the manipulation of constituency boundaries for party political advantage, is a clear form of political corruption. So, too, would be any misuse of municipal powers, intended for use in the general public interest but used instead for party political advantage. Who can doubt that the selective use of municipal powers in order to obtain party political advantage represents political corruption? Political corruption, if unchecked, engenders cynicism about elections, about politicians and and their motives and damages the reputation of democratic government. Like Viola's 'worm i' the bud' it feeds upon democratic institutions from within (*Twelfth Night*).[17]

Viola's use of the phrase occurs in her response to Duke Orsino's query regarding the history of that daughter of her father's who had loved a man. Viola, disguised as the page Cesario and who is eventually to marry Orsino, responded:

> She never told her love,
> But let concealment, like a worm i' the bud,
> Feed on her damask cheek: she pined in thought;
> And with a green and yellow melancholy
> She sat like patience on a monument,
> Smiling at grief.[18]

A WINTER'S TALE

In *Bagot v. Bagot*, an Irish probate action heard in 1878,[19] Mr Justice Warren was faced with the problem as to whether the testator, when he signed a will disinheriting his infant son, was under an insane delusion that the child was not

16 [2002] 2 AC at 503. **17** *Twelfth Night*, act 2, scene 4, line 114. **18** *Twelfth Night*, act 2, scene 4, lines 113–18. **19** 1 LR Ir 308.

his. Inevitably, the paternity of the child became an issue. Two witnesses gave evidence of a paternal resemblance between the child and his supposed father. A medical witness swore 'the child was very like the deceased – there is a broad resemblance; he is totally different from his mother, and very like his father.'[20] A second witness declared:

> When I saw Mr Bagot sitting in the chair, and beside him the child, I was very struck by the likeness; there was an unmistakable resemblance. I said, 'The child is remarkably like you.'[21]

A verdict against the will was pronounced, and an application for a new trial followed. This Mr Justice Warren turned down, upholding the decision to admit this evidence, which had critically influenced the original verdict.

'Was this evidence illegal?', the judge asked rhetorically.[22] There was an amount of legal authority, which the judge was to rehearse, that gave a negative answer to that question.[23] Had there been none, he would have been prepared to admit as authority even so what had been cited in argument by the solicitor-general, Gerald FitzGibbon, when supporting the original verdict and opposing the motion for a new trial.

These were two passages from *A winter's tale* which the Irish Reports were to conveniently supply in a footnote.[24]

The first passage is from act 2, scene 3 (lines 92–107), and finds Leontes, King of Sicilia, and Paulina discussing the self-same problem as was to present itself in *Bagot v. Bagot*:

> LEONTES This brat is none of mine;
> It is the issue of Polixenes:
> Hence with it; and, together with the dam,
> Commit them to the fire!
> PAULINA It is yours;
> And, might we lay the old proverb to your charge,
> So like you, 'tis the worse. Behold, my lords,
> Although the print be little, the whole matter
> And copy of the father, eye, nose, lip;
> The trick of 's frown; his forehead; nay, the valley,
> The pretty dimples of his chin and cheek; his smiles;
> The very mould and frame of hand, nail, finger:

20 1 LR Ir at 308. **21** Ibid. **22** 1 LR Ir at 311. **23** Ibid., at 312. **24** 1 LR Ir at 311–12.

And thou, good goddess Nature, which hast made it
So like to him that got it, if thou hast
The ordering of the mind too, 'mongst all colours
No yellow in 't; lest she suspect, as he does,
Her children, not her husband's!

And the second passage is from a rather different speech of Leontes in act 5, scene 1 (lines 124–9), where the King of Sicilia addresses Prince Florizel:

Your mother was most true to wedlock, prince;
For she did print your royal father off,
Conceiving you: were I but twenty one,
Your father's image is so hit in you,
His very air, that I should call you brother,
As I did him.

This, however, was not to be the last word on *Bagot v. Bagot*, the Court of Appeal ultimately granting a motion for a new trial on an entirely separate point.[25]

25 *Bagot v. Bagot* (1879) 5 LR Ir 72.

CHAPTER 5

Seventeenth and eighteenth centuries

BEN JONSON
*c.*1572–1637

See above, p. 60.

PHILIP MASSINGER
1583–1640

The background to the Irish defamation action of *McInerney v. Clareman Printing and Publishing Co.*[1] has previously been given (see above, pp 17–19). As is there recalled, in the Court of Appeal Lord Justice Holmes exonerated Mr Justice Gibson from his failure to explain to the special jury that heard the action the possible meanings of the term 'land-grabber'. 'Mr Justice Gibson was right', Lord Justice Holmes claimed,[2]

> in not embarrassing the case with innuendoes. 'Land-grabbing' and a 'land-grabber' are familiar words to Irish ears, and their meaning is well understood.

The idea, he continued, was neither novel nor peculiar to Ireland, and a citation from Isaiah was furnished in confirmation. The reference to Philip Massinger then follows:[3]

> ... and Massinger in his best known comedy held up to odium the man who 'to increase possessions and annual rents' had all men sellers and himself the only purchaser.

The allusion here is to Massinger's 'A new way to pay old debts'[4] and to the character Sir Giles Overreach. Overreach's villainy is best captured in dialogue between Marrall and Overreach early in act 2 of the comedy:[5]

1 [1903] 2 IR 347. 2 At 402. 3 Ibid. 4 See, conveniently, *The plays and poems of Philip Massinger, vol. 2*, ed. Philip Edwards and Colin Gibson (Oxford, 1976). 5 Act 2, scene 1, lines 26–42, 44–8. It is claimed that Overreach's character was based by Massinger on the equally unscrupulous Sir Giles Mompesson.

MARRALL: What course take you,
With your good patience, to hedge in the Mannour
Of your neighbour master Frugall? as 'tis sayd,
He will not sell, nor borrow, nor exchange,
And his land lying in the midst of your many Lordshipps,
Is a foule blemish.
OVERREACH: I have thought on't, Marrall,
And it shall take. I must have all men sellers,
And I the only Purchaser.
MARRALL: 'Tis most fit Sir.
OVERREACH: I'll therefore buy some Cottage near his Mannour,
Which done, I'll make my men brake ope his fences;
Ride o're his standing corne, and in the night
Set fire on his barnes; or breake his cattells legges.
These Trespasses draw on Suites, and Suites expences,
Which I can spare, but will soone begger Him.
When I have harried him this two, or three yeare,
Though he sue *in forma pauperis*, in spite
Of all his thrift and care he'll grow behind-hand.
...
Then with the favour of my man of Law,
I will pretend some title: Want will force him
To put it to arbitrement: then if he sell
For halfe the value, he shall have ready money,
And I possesse his land.

FRANCIS BEAUMONT
1584–1616

See above, p. 60.

ISAAK WALTON
1593–1683

A pleasing flourish from Lord Hailsham as lord chancellor concluded his speech in the House of Lords at the hearing of an appeal in which it was claimed that a lease had been frustrated, so rent had been properly withheld.[6]

6 *National Carriers Ltd. v. Panalpina (Northern) Ltd.* [1981] AC 675.

Panalpina (Northern) Ltd. had demised to them for ten years a warehouse. Five years into the lease, the local authority closed the only means of vehicular access to and from the warehouse, because of the dangerous condition of a derelict Victorian warehouse opposite to Panalpina's. In theory, the House of Lords was to hold, the doctrine of frustration was applicable to leases. In the instant case, however, having regard in particular to the likely length of continuance of the lease after the interruption of user, on the facts Panalpina had failed to raise a triable issue as to the doctrine's applicability.

At the conclusion of his speech Lord Hailsham observed that he had been impressed by the fact that there appeared to be no English case in the reports where a lease had ever been held to have been frustrated.[7] This spawned an aside, to which plainly it was intended proper weight should be given. 'I hope this fact', Lord Hailsham continues,[8]

> will act as a suitable deterrent to the litigious, eager to make legal history by being first in this field. But I am comforted by the implications of the well known passage in *The compleat angler* (pt. 1, ch. 5) on the subject of strawberries: 'Doubtless God could have made a better berry, but doubtless God never did.'[9] I only append to this observation of nature the comment that it does not follow from these premises that He never will, and if it does not follow, an assumption that He never will becomes exceedingly rash.[10]

In recent days the reputation of certain kinds of strawberry, it needs to be said, has suffered – much, one would imagine, to the dismay of the author of *The compleat angler*. The draping of vast sheets of polythene over acre upon acre of strawberry plants in order to prolong the growing season, as well as distracting from the aesthetic enjoyment of the countryside has been reckoned to have caused a deterioration in the quality of 'the best of berries'. In an editorial in the *Daily Telegraph* in June 2006 'war' was proclaimed against the unseasonal produce of the polytunnels, especially those in Herefordshire:[11]

> These polythene arches, plastering the countryside and lowering house prices, often provide extremely unappetising fruit – swollen, crunchy and flavourless. The head chef of the Savoy, no less, has banned them.

7 [1981] AC at 692. 8 Ibid. 9 Izaak Walton, *The compleat angler* (Everyman ed., London, 1906), p. 100 (The Fourth Day). Piscator in this dialogue with Venator attributes the saying to Dr Boteler. 10 The additional comment from Piscator in *The compleat angler* might be compared: 'and so, if I might be judge, God never did make a more calm, quiet, innocent recreation than angling'. 11 *Daily Telegraph*, 6 June 2006.

JOHN MILTON
1612–1680

In 1870 the Scots judge, Lord Ardmillan, along with his colleagues in the 1st Division of the Court of Session, was obliged to resolve a dispute concerning title to a hearse that had been constructed partly of materials supplied by *A* and partly of materials supplied by *B*.[12] The problem was immediately identified, quite correctly, as one in the *specificatio* of Roman law. Lord Ardmillan paused to refer 'to the celebrated controversy between the Proculeians and the Sabinians', but indicated that he did not propose 'to enter on that alarming field of judicial conflict'.[13] Milton came to mind, as the judge added that he shrank in fact from even treading on the edge of

> ... that Serbonian bog,
> Betwixt Damiata and Mount Casius old,
> Where armies whole have sunk.[14]

*

The killing in the Indian Ocean many hundreds of miles from land of the cabin boy, one Brooks, by Thomas Dudley and Edward Stephens, after all three had been seven days without food and five without water gave rise, as is well known, to a celebrated trial for murder.[15] The remains of a turtle having been finally consumed, the two older crew members resolved on Brooks's death, so that they could at least exist on his flesh against the prospect of their eventual rescue. The trial jury at the Devon and Cornwall assizes in November 1884 returned a special verdict which led to the entire case being argued before five judges of the Queen's Bench Division a month later. The court unanimously held that a man who, in order to escape death from hunger, killed another for the purpose of eating his flesh, was guilty of murder. The court specifically rejected the availability, on the facts of the case, of any defence of necessity.

Lord Coleridge CJ was especially perturbed at the fact that on board the open boat 'the weakest, the youngest, the most unresisting, was chosen'.[16] 'Was it

12 *Wylie and Lochhead v. Mitchell* (1870) 8 Macph. 552. 13 8 Macph. at 561. See further D.G. Osler, '*Specificatio* in Scots law' in R. Evans-Jones (ed.), *The civil law tradition in Scots law* (Edinburgh, 1995), p. 100. 14 'Paradise Lost', book 2, lines 592–4. Serbonis was a lake bordered by quicksands on the Egyptian coast; Damiata (east of the Nile) and Mt. Casius were both names occurring in Italian epics. See further, *The poems of John Milton*, ed. John Carey and Alastair Fowler (London, 1968), p. 535. 15 *The Queen v. Dudley and Stephens* (1884) 14 QBD 273. 16 14 QBD at 287–8.

more necessary to kill him than one of the grown men?' His negative response to his own rhetorical question is succeeded by a quotation from Milton:[17]

> So spoke the Fiend, and with necessity,
> The tyrant's plea, excused his devilish deeds.[18]

Dudley and Stephens were subsequently sentenced to death for murder, but this sentence was afterwards commuted to six months imprisonment.[19]

Strabo in his *Geography* alludes to recorded instances in history of besieged inhabitants resorting to cannibalism.[20] Valerius Maximus furnishes more detail on one of these instances, when Numantia in Spain was besieged by Scipio. Valerius Maximus's disapproval is announced in terms that anticipate the lines in Milton:[21]

> Nulla est in his necessitatis excusatio: nam quibus mori licuit, sic vivere necesse non fuit.
>
> Here necessity is no excuse. For people who were free to die, it was not necessary to live thus.

*

In book 9 of 'Paradise Lost' we follow the serpent in the Garden of Eden as he plots the downfall of man, 'his purposed prey'. Cunning strategist that he was, he planned to confront Adam and Eve together. Preferably, however, he might find Eve by herself and proceed to the temptation of her alone. This he accepted was unlikely, it was something that 'so seldom chanc'd'. But the serpent was in for a surprise. 'When to his wish', Milton tells us,[22]

> Beyond his hope, Eve separate he spies.

It was indeed an extraordinary stroke of luck. Eve's vulnerability contrasted with the image we are given of her. 'Veild in a Cloud of Fragrance, where she stood', Milton writes,[23]

17 14 QBD at 288. 18 'Paradise Lost', book 4, lines 393–4. 19 14 QBD at 288. See further A.W.B. Simpson, *Cannibalism and the common law* (London, 1986). 20 *The geography of Strabo*, 4.5.4. 21 Valerius Maximus, *Memorable doings and sayings*, ed. and trans. D.R. Shackleton Bailey, 2 vols. (Cambridge, MA, and London, 2000), ii, 168–71. 22 Book 9, lines 423–4. 23 Ibid., lines 425–33.

Half spi'd, so thick the Roses bushing round
About her glowd, oft stooping to support
Each Flour of slender stalk, whose head though gay
Carnation, Purple, Azure, or spect with Gold,
Hung drooping unsustained, them she upstaies
Gently with Mirtle band, mindless the while,
Her self, though fairest unsupported Flour,
From her best prop so farr, and storm so nigh.

The words that introduce the serpent's discovery of Eve – the passage running from 'When to his wish' to 'Eve separate he spies' – are included by Mr Turner, QC in that part of his argument in the Gorham appeal (*Gorham v. Bishop of Exeter*)[24] where he conducts his disquisition on the meaning of the word 'hope' ('spes' in the Latin). See further the entries on THE BIBLE (*Job*) (pp 16–17) and on SALLUST (pp 41–2).

*

Sophia Louise Jex-Blake in 1873 fought an ultimately unsuccessful battle to graduate as a woman doctor in the University of Edinburgh: *Jex-Blake v. Senatus of University of Edinburgh*.[25] Not that, as a biography published shortly after her death occurring in 1912 was to show, that prevented her from fulfilling her life's ambition.[26] The university had permitted her to matriculate and had arranged for women medical students to be instructed separately. Certain professors, however, refused to put on such separate classes as envisaged, with the result that Miss Jex-Blake could not complete the course prescribed for the award of medical degrees and so was debarred from practising the medical profession. Miss Jex-Blake's action was designed to force the hand of the university authorities.

The lord ordinary, Lord Gifford, was prepared to rule in Miss Jex-Blake's favour,[27] but at the appeal a majority in the Court of Session (Second Division) overruled his decision. It added fuel to the fire when that majority also held that the decision to allow women to be matriculated was ultra vires the university.

There is much of interest in the judgments of each of the judges – both 'the consulted judges' and 'at the advising'. Among the judges of the majority (Lords Ormidale, Mure, Mackenzie, Shand, Cowan, Benholme and Neaves), it is the

24 89 RR at 729n. 25 (1873) 11 Macph. 784. 26 M.G. Todd, *Life of Sophia Jex-Blake* (London, 1918). 27 11 Macph. at 792 ff.

judgment of the last of these – Lord Neaves – that perhaps stands out.[28] It possesses the largest number of quotable passages. Girding his loins, in preparation for the conclusion that will be adverse to Miss Jex-Blake, Lord Neaves pens lines on the purpose as he saw it of higher education in Scotland. 'The Universities of Scotland', he argues,[29]

> were instituted and maintained for the special and exclusive purpose of conferring the benefits of the higher education upon male students without the necessity of their resorting for that purpose to foreign countries.

The converting of 'a little state into a great one' – the underlying objective – had been attained, Neaves writes,[30]

> attained mainly, as I can conceive, by means of those great educational arrangements which were designed to produce able, learned, and accomplished men, for the salvation of the state and the advancement of the public welfare, – learned and able divines for the service of religion, learned and able lawyers for the practice of the law, skilful and enlightened magistrates and judges for the administration of justice, and wise and prudent politicians and statesmen for the great purposes of national legislation.

An apt quotation from Milton's great essay 'On Education' concludes this opening paragraph in Lord Neaves's judgment:[31]

> The purpose, I take it, was to confer a complete and generous education, which Milton has defined to be 'that which fits a man to perform justly, skilfully, and magnanimously all the offices, both private and public, of peace and war'.[32]

Neaves goes on to quote Roman law, 'the great parent of our own legal system', which denied women a role in public life, least of all in law, as judges or practitioners:[33]

> Feminae ab omnibus officiis civilibus vel publicis remotae sunt: et ideo, nec judices esse possunt, nec magistratum gerere, nec postulare, nec pro alio intervenire nec procuratores existere.

28 11 Macph. at 831–7. 29 Ibid., at 831. 30 Ibid. 31 Ibid. 32 'Of Education to Master Samuel Hartlib': see, conveniently, *The works of John Milton*, vol. 4 (New York, 1931), p. 273 at p. 280. 33 11 Macph. at 832.

He does find time, however, to dwell on the perils of mixed university education:[34]

> The period of life attained by the youth who are there educated, say from sixteen to twenty-two, is the most of all susceptible of the more tender feelings of our nature; and, without the slightest suggestion of anything in the least degree culpable, how is it possible to feel secure that, with a number of young men and women assembled together at a University, there shall not occur hasty attachments and premature entanglements, that may exercise a blighting influence on all their future life? What effect it might exercise upon their immediate studies it would be hazardous to conjecture. It might, in some cases, produce a strange emulation; it might in others lead to total idleness among these mixed schoolfellows. In any view, he would be a bold man who would collect together at a College, and send out some hundreds of young men and women
>
> Inter sylvas Academi quaerere verum,
>
> with whatever number of chaperons he might try to guard them.

In light of this passage, it may be remarked in parenthesis, it is perhaps a little difficult, prima facie at least, to express concurrence with the judgment on Lord Neaves, to be found in the *Oxford dictionary of national biography*,[35] that he was 'reputedly well disposed towards the movement for the teaching of women at universities'.

SAMUEL BUTLER
1612–1680

In *Wise v. Dunning* in 1901[36] the King's Bench Division in England agreed that, in the circumstances of the case, the Liverpool stipendiary magistrate had jurisdiction to bind Wise over in recognizances to be of good behaviour. Wise, described as a Protestant lecturer, had held meetings in public places in Liverpool that had caused large crowds to assemble and to obstruct the thoroughfare. More to the point, Wise in his address at these meetings had used gestures and language likely to be regarded as highly insulting by the substantial Roman Catholic population. At one of the meetings Wise had apparently told

34 11 Macph. at 834. 35 *Oxford dictionary of national biography*, 60 vols. (Oxford, 2004), vol 40, p. 313. 36 [1902] 1 KB 167.

his supporters that he had been informed that the Catholics were going to bring sticks; and, on some of his supporters saying that they would bring sticks too, he said he looked to them for protection. Mr Justice Darling called Samuel Butler in aid in producing his thumbnail sketch of Wise included in his judgment:[37]

> The kind of person which the evidence here shews the appellant to be I can best describe in the language of Butler. He is one of
>
> … that stubborn Crew
> of Errant Saints, whom all men grant
> To be the true Church Militant:
> …
> A Sect, whose chief Devotion lies
> In odde perverse Antipathies.[38]

JONATHAN SWIFT
1667–1754

On 11 November 1938 the Roslevan School in Athlone was destroyed by a fire which had spread to it from the adjoining premises. These were the premises of the Athlone Woollen Mills in which the fire had originated. In the ensuing legal proceedings commenced by the owners of the school, the question arose as to whether the proprietors of the mills were exonerated from liability under the terms of the Irish Accidental Fires Act of 1715[39] (an Act for preventing mischiefs that may happen by fire). Section 1 of this legislation provided that 'no action, suit or process whatsoever shall be had, maintained, or prosecuted against any person or persons in whose house or chamber any fire shall … accidentally begin'. In *Richardson and Webster v. Athlone Woollen Mills*,[40] the trial judge, Mr Justice Maguire, president of the High Court, ruled that the mills fell within the exemption, but the Supreme Court unanimously overturned that interpretation: a factory for purposes of the 1715 Act was neither a 'house' nor a 'chamber'. Some doubt attached to the meaning of the word 'chamber', but Mr Justice O'Byrne in his judgment in the Supreme Court was satisfied that it meant a room or apartment in a house, usually appropriated to the use of one person, especially a sleeping apartment or a bedroom.[41] It was used, the judge

37 Ibid., at 178. 38 'Hudibras', First part, canto I, lines 190–2, 205–6. 39 2 Geo. I, c. 5. 40 [1942] IR 581. 41 [1942] IR at 593–4.

continued, in this sense by Swift in 1711, four years before the Accidental Fires Act was passed. He took it therefore to be a well recognised meaning of the term at the time when the Act was adopted.[42]

ALAIN-RENÉ LESAGE
1668–1747

In all centuries, Lord Anderson averred in his account of the inn in history (see above, p. 55), the principal functions of the inn had been to furnish rest and refreshment for the traveller.[43] 'The writings of Le Sage and Cervantes as to Spanish inns ... make this quite clear.'[44] Italian and French authors concurred.

JOHN GAY
1685–1732

In *In re Pickworth*, in the late 1880s,[45] first Mr Justice North and then the Court of Appeal resolved a problem presented by the will of one Maria Pickworth. Maria, by her will of 1872, gave residuary trust moneys upon trust to pay the interest to her sister Thirza during her life, and after her death to pay and divide the said trust moneys equally between two other sisters, Frances and Sarah, share and share alike. There then followed the critical stipulation that gave rise to the difficulty in the case. 'And if either of my said sisters' – meaning Frances and Sarah – 'shall be then dead ... upon trust for the survivor of my said sisters absolutely'. Thirza, who was entitled to the life interest in the fund, died in 1897, outliving both of the other sisters, Sarah dying in 1886 and Frances in 1891. The question then arose as to whether the legal personal representatives of Frances, the survivor of the two legatees, were entitled to the whole of the residuary estate of Maria or whether they and the legal personal representatives of Sarah were entitled to that estate in equal shares. Mr Justice North held that there was no surviving sister when Thirza died, both then being dead, and that the clear original gift to Frances and Sarah as tenants in common was not divested.[46] The Court of Appeal, by a majority (Lord Lindley, the master of the rolls, and Lord Justice Vaughan Williams; Lord Justice Rigby dissenting), agreed.

The last two paragraphs of the judgment of Lord Justice Vaughan Williams

42 Ibid., at 594. 43 *Rothfield v. North British Ry. Co.*, 1920 SC 805. 44 At 816. 45 [1899] 1 Ch. 642. 46 Ibid.

are given over to a detailed discussion of the meaning of the word 'either' and its difference from the word 'both'.

'It was', the judge observed,[47] 'a question rather of grammar than of law'. As an illustration of his meaning he then proceeded to cite a passage from *The beggar's opera.*[48] It is Macheath who is speaking:

> How happy could I be with either,
> Were t'other dear charmer away;
> But now you both tease me together,[49]
> To neither a word will I say.

Our judicial pedagogue continued:[50]

> However possible it might be, if you left out the last three lines, to treat the word 'either' as meaning both, the real reason why you cannot treat it as meaning both in that sentence is, not only the obvious meaning of Captain Macheath when he used the words, but because it comes within the rule that I have stated that you find in the predicate which is applied to this subject that the two are treated in opposition and separately, and when that is so you ought not in the subject part of the sentence to treat the word 'either' as meaning 'both'.

Thus were matters clarified.

In a different context altogether, it is perhaps easier to grasp the difference between 'both' and 'either'. In an issue of the *Daily Telegraph* in November 2006,[51] a correspondent voiced objection to one road sign designed to improve the flow of traffic. The sign read: 'Use both lanes'. On one interpretation, wide vehicles alone could oblige. It was better – more accurate, too, in fact – if the sign read: 'use either lane'.

A final footnote is worth adding. The very lines from *The beggar's opera* quoted by Lord Justice Vaughan Williams in *In re Pickworth* are repeated in *Kind hearts and coronets* by the wrongly pardoned duke of Chalfont, played in the Ealing Films version of the tale by Denis Price.[52]

Chalfont on his release from prison ponders the need to make a choice between the two women in his life, Edith (Valerie Hobson) and the dangerous

47 [1899] 1 Ch. at 654–55. 48 Act 2, sc. 13, lines 33–36 (air xxxv): *The poetical works of John Gay*, ed. G.C. Faber (New York, 1926), p. 514. 49 Faber's edition (above) gives this line as 'But while you thus teaze me together'. 50 [1899] 1 Ch. at 655. 51 13 November 2006. 52 The film was based on the novel by Roy Horniman.

Sibella (Joan Greenwood), to each of whom a certain commitment had been made:

> How happy could I be with either,
> Were t'other dear charmer away.

The ultimate scene from the screenplay would suggest, however, that time was running out for the duke who had murdered his way through the Gascoyne heirs (all played in the film by Alec Guinness) to secure the inheritance to the dukedom, and might not therefore find himself in a position where he had to make a choice at all. As much was confessed in Chalfont's memoirs which he had absentmindedly left behind in the death cell. If the prison authorities were to invade his privacy and peruse the volume …

ALEXANDER POPE
1688–1744

The secrecy that attaches to the deliberations of the jury constitutes a constant refrain in modern criminal procedure caselaw. It entails that allegations of any irregularity supposed to have occurred will be given short shrift, with one key consequence – such allegations furnish no grounds for setting aside any criminal conviction brought in by the particular jury in question. The rule has struck certain observers as too draconian, and it was perhaps no surprise that in 2004 the House of Lords embarked on a fresh consideration of it. Two cases were considered together: *R. v. Mirza* and *R. v. Connor and Rollock.*[53] Lord Rodger of Earlsferry chose in his judgment in the two cases to set out some of the factors that could well dispose any jury to discharge their functions in a less than acceptable fashion. 'Some', he argued,[54]

> may be affected by religious bias, others may make it a rule always to believe an Irishman but never to trust a Scotsman, others again will never trust a man in a suit or a woman in trousers, while still others may be predisposed to believe anything – or nothing – that a police officer says.

In the case of Connor and Rollock the allegation, contained in a letter forwarded by a member of the jury after the trial, was to the effect that the jury

53 [2004] 1 AC 1118. 54 [2004] 1 AC at 1174.

had chosen the easy way out by convicting both defendants of the offence of wounding as an alternative to spending time deliberating on the individual guilt of the two men.[55] For Lord Rodger this was a classic case of what had been warned against by Alexander Pope in his mock heroic poem 'The rape of the lock': 'And Wretches hang that Jurymen may Dine'.[56] This is the line that immediately follows another, expressive of a sentiment equally to be disowned: 'The hungry Judges soon the Sentence sign'.[57]

Earlier in the same canto in 'The rape of the lock', where the focus is on the royal residence of Hampton Court, Pope produced another two memorable lines, apropos, on this occasion, Queen Anne:[58]

> Here Thou, Great Anna! whom three Realms obey
> Dost sometimes Counsel take – and sometimes Tea.

The decision the House of Lords reached in the two cases before it is not, naturally, without interest. The House of Lords held that a court could in theory investigate allegations of jury misconduct – to ensure that the trial itself had been 'fair'- but, in all the circumstances of the two cases, went on to conclude that the allegations raised by the juror in each were not admissible. In short, viewing the prodeedings as a whole, none of the defendants had received an unfair trial. There was to be a partial dissent from Lord Steyn in the result, allowing the appeal in the case of Mirza but turning it down in that of Connor and Rollock.[59]

MONTESQUIEU
Charles de Secondat, Baron de Montesquieu
1689–1755

A regulation made in Britain under the First World War Defence of the Realm Regulations[60] sought to protect the residence rights of munitions workers. It provided that no person should 'without the consent of the Minister of

55 In the *Mirza* case the complaining letter from the juror after the trial alleged that other jurors had been prejudiced against the defendant on racial grounds. 56 Canto III, line 21: *The poems of Alexander Pope*, ed. John Butt (London and New York, 1992), p. 227; [2004] 1 AC at 1175: 'Alexander Pope skewered that type of abuse almost 300 years ago in his chilling remark'. 57 Canto III, line 22. 58 Canto III, lines 7–8. 59 The panel that sat to hear the cases comprised Lord Steyn, Lord Slynn of Hadley, Lord Hope of Craighead, Lord Hobhouse of Woodborough and Lord Rodger of Earlsferry. 60 Reg. 2A (2).

Munitions take ... any proceedings for the purpose of obtaining an order or decree for the recovery of, or for the ejectment of a tenant of, any dwelling-house' in which a munitions worker was living, and which was situate in an area declared by order of the minister to be a 'special area'. When a landlord, one Chester, in such a special area in Lancashire sought to recover possession of certain premises, the tenant, one Bateson, objected that the procedure laid down in the regulation requiring that ministerial permission be first obtained had not been followed and that the complaint preferred by the landlord was otiose. The tenant pointed out that he was employed in the shell shop at Messrs Vickers, Ltd., at Barrow-in-Furness, where he was engaged in checking the loading and unloading of shells, shell material and shell forgings.[61]

The justices before whom the complaint was presented held that the critical regulation was not ultra vires and that it was essential therefore that before proceedings by the landlord could be taken, he should first obtain the consent of the minister. This had not occurred.

On a case stated, a unanimous King's Bench Division (Mr Justice Darling, Mr Justice Avery and Mr Justice Sankey) ruled that the justices were in error, as in their opinion, the regulation in question was not authorised by the enabling legislation, the Defence of the Realm Consolidation Act 1914,[62] and it was therefore invalid.[63]

The leading judgment was delivered by Mr Justice Darling, who employed the occasion to defend the right of unfettered access to the courts and, in the process, to quote from Montesquieu's *De l'esprit des lois*. 'It is to be observed,' Mr Justice Darling begins,[64]

> that this regulation not only deprives the subject of his ordinary right to seek justice in the Courts of law, but provides that merely to resort there without the permission of the Minister of Munitions first had and obtained shall of itself be a summary offence, and so render the seeker after justice liable to imprisonment and fine.

More follows. 'I allow', he continues,[65]

> that in stress of war we may rightly be obliged, as we should be ready, to forgo much of our liberty, but I hold that this elemental right of the subjects of the British Crown cannot be thus easily taken from them.

61 For these details see *Chester v. Bateson* [1920] 1 KB 829 at 830. 62 5 Geo. V, c. 8. 63 *Chester v. Bateson* [1920] 1 KB 829. 64 Ibid., at 834. 65 Ibid.

Should we hold that the permit of a departmental official is a necessary condition precedent for a subject of the realm who would demand justice at the seat of judgment the people would be in that unhappy condition indicated, but not anticipated, by Montesquieu, in *De l'Esprit des Lois* where he writes:

> Les Anglais pour favoriser la liberté ont ôté toutes les puissances intermédiaires qui formoient leur monarchie. Ils ont bien raison de conserver cette liberté; s'ils venoient à la perdre, ils seroient un des peuples les plus esclaves de la terre.
>
> (Livre 2, c. 4).

Montesquieu's observations on the English and their constitution are generally favourable. There is occasionally, however, a sour note sounded. One such will be found in his *Pensées diverses*: 'Les Anglais sont occupés; ils n'ont pas de temps d'être polis.'

HENRY FIELDING
1707–1754

With the establishment of stage-coach routes and the consequential increase in numbers of the travelling public, furnishing accommodation for such travellers became more manifestly 'the main business of the innkeeper'.[66] Thus the Scots judge, Lord Anderson, in his essay on the inn in history (for the background to this essay see above, p. 55). 'The writings of Fielding and Smollett', the judge continued, 'show how this was done in England and Scotland'.[67]

SAMUEL JOHNSON
1707–1784

In the recital of facts presented by Mr Justice Buckley in his judgment in the Restrictive Practices Court upholding the validity of the Net Book Agreement,[68] space is given to the matter of booksellers' profits. Dr Johnson's views on booksellers as a class were to be noted in the judge's conclusions on the

66 *Rothfield v. North British Ry. Co.*, 1920 SC 805 at 816. 67 Ibid. 68 *In re Net Book Agreement 1957* (1963) LR 3 RP 246, [1962] 1 WLR 1347.

opportunities for wealth-making in this area of the book trade. 'The net profits earned by booksellers in this country', Mr Justice Buckley reported,[69]

> are modest compared with those earned in most other commercial fields. This is not because, as Dr Johnson found,[70] 'book sellers are generous, liberal-minded men', but because in the competitive state of the book trade publishers have so far been able to resist pressure by booksellers for higher rates of discount.

*

In modern times Lord Anderson was to write in his extended essay on the inn in history (for the background to which see above, p. 55), inns came to be employed for a novel purpose: they would be used 'as meeting places by local residents who were socially inclined'.[71] 'It was this feature of inn life', the judge went on, 'which attracted Dr Johnson to "The Mitre".'[72]

THOMAS GRAY
1716–1771

There is a short allusion to 'The elegy written in a country churchyard' in a passage in Mr Justice Buckley's judgment of 1962 in the Restrictive Practices Court upholding the validity of the Net Book Agreement.[73] Abolition of the agreement, the judge argued, would create more hazardous conditions in the world of book publishing and many authors would not find a publisher at all.[74] 'We cannot doubt', he continued, 'that this would deny to the reading public specific and substantial benefits'. The point merited emphasis, at least the judge so reckoned. He went on:

> It is improbable that there are many 'mute inglorious Miltons' about nowadays, but there may be a few, and the likelihood of their muteness would be increased if publishers were constrained to be less adventurous.

69 [1962] 1 WLR at 1361. 70 The reference the judge gives is to Boswell's *Life of Johnson*, ed. J.W. Cooper (London, 1860), p. 100. 71 *Rothfield v. North British Ry. Co.*, 1920 SC 805 at 817. 72 Ibid. 73 *In re Net Book Agreement 1957* (1963) LR 3 RP 246, [1962] 1 WLR 1347. 74 [1962] 1 WLR at 1386.

TOBIAS GEORGE SMOLLETT
1721–1771

With the inauguration of stage-coach routes and the predictable increase in the numbers of those travelling, furnishing accommodation for such travellers became self-evidently 'the main business of the innkeeper'.[75] Thus Lord Anderson, the Scots judge, in his discourse on the inn in history (for the background to the composition of which, see above, p. 55). 'The writings of Fielding and Smollett', the judge added, 'show how this was done in England and Scotland'.[76]

JOHANN WOLFGANG VON GOETHE
1749–1832

In a South African rape case, reported in 1953,[77] the question raised, as so often in such cases, was whether or not the woman had consented. Van den Heever J.A. went into the matter at a little length. Evidence of crying after instances of intercourse would be difficult to interpret. 'Tears after the event,' the judge declared,[78]

> are not necessarily indications of absence of consent. They may be tears of remorse or apprehension. Gretchen's famous lament is no pointer to her having been ravished by Faust.

For much of the recent past, Goethe's Faust, as one critic was to express it,[79] had been regarded 'outside the world of scholarship, as the embodiment of titanic despair and as the infamous lover of Gretchen'. This is simple enough to understand, though the aptness of Judge Van den Heever's allusion to Gretchen's lament less easily so, for Gretchen (Margarete) was, is, and always will be, tragedy writ large. Seduced by Faust, through the machinations of Mephistopheles and the use of a sleeping draught, she is later abandoned by her seducer. Much worse follows. She kills the child she bears and is sentenced to death for infanticide. Faust eventually returns with a plan to rescue her from the condemned cell, but, like Socrates, Gretchen forgoes the opportunity to escape. That cell Gretchen had come to regard as a sanctuary where she could condemn

75 *Rothfield v. North British Ry. Co.*, 1920 SC 805 at 816. 76 Ibid. 77 *R. v. M.*, 1953 (4) SA 393. 78 Ibid., at 397. 79 Alexander Gillies, *Goethe's Faust: an interpretation* (Oxford, 1957), p. 3.

herself 'to God's justice and to it alone and accept death as a step towards salvation'.[80]

ROBERT BURNS
1759–1796

In *In re O'Hara*[81] the Irish Court of Appeal reversed Mr Justice Kenny and ordered the return of Harriet O'Hara, then 11 years old, to her mother and stepfather. Due to the penurious circumstances of the mother, Harriet had two years before been entrusted to the care of a family called McMahon. Having remarried and gained a modicum of wealth, she had to resort to a writ of *habeas corpus* to secure Harriet's return into the family fold. Though Mr Justice Kenny had decided otherwise, the Court of Appeal was satisfied that the right thing to do was to insist that Harriet leave the McMahons. Lord Justice Holmes was in no doubt about the matter even if the McMahons could lay claim to rather more in the way of this world's goods. An allusion to Robert Burns's childhood and the benefits thereby incurred found Holmes in philosophical mood. 'It would be more for the welfare of this child', he observed,[82]

> to be with her mother and stepfather. But even if this were otherwise, even if she would be somewhat better off if left with the McMahons, I should still hold that it is for her welfare, as that term is understood and explained by illustrious Judges, to place her under her mother's care. There are dark shadows in every life. Neither the farmer's nor the peasant's child is free from trouble ... The greatest of Scottish poets, recalling probably his own childhood spent in a mud hovel built with his father's hands, has given the world a picture of the cotter's home when the labours of the week are ended, made beautiful by unity and mutual loyalty.

*

In recent centuries, the Scots judge Lord Anderson was to affirm in 1920, in his extended essay on the inn in history (for the background to which see above, p. 55), inns came to be employed for a novel function: they would be used 'as meeting places, by local residents who were socially inclined'.[83] It was this

80 Ibid., p. 94. 81 [1900] 2 IR 232. 82 At 256–7. 83 *Rothfield v. North British Ry. Co.*, 1920 SC 805 at 817.

feature of inn life, Lord Anderson saw fit to add, 'which attracted ... Robert Burns to "Poosie Nancie's" and other taverns'.[84]

*

In 1966 a Mr Zesko, a Polish national living in London, applied to be placed on the housing list maintained by the pertinent local authority, Ealing London Borough Council.[85] The latter had adopted a rule to the effect that any such applicant had to be 'a British subject within the meaning of the British Nationality Act 1948'; Mr Zesko accordingly was not placed on the housing list, despite the fact that, as appears to have been agreed, Mr Zesko who after service with the Royal Air Force during World War II worked as 'a glass toughener', and was 'a man of perfect character and integrity and a wholly admirable person'. He and his wife had one child, born in 1960.[86] After the Race Relations Act 1968 came into effect, Mr Zesko lodged a complaint over his being denied a place on Ealing's housing list. He argued that that denial constituted discrimination against him on the ground of his 'national origins' contrary to section 1 (i) and 5(c) of the Act of 1968. The Race Relations Board upheld his complaint.

Two issues surfaced in the resultant appeals, first to the High Court and then to the House of Lords. First, did the Act of 1968 oust the jurisdiction of the courts in such cases? And what was the meaning of the phrase 'national origins'? The House of Lords agreed with the High Court judge, Mr Justice Swanwick,[87] that the scheme of the 1968 Act did not preclude the involvement of the courts. But, secondly, they held that 'national' in 'national origins' in section 1(i) of the Act meant national in the sense of race and not citizenship, and that, accordingly, the Ealing Council had not acted unlawfully in declining to enter Mr Zesko's name on their housing list.

The difficulty with the phrase 'national origins' and the word 'national' provoked, in the case of Lord Simon of Glaisdale, a long excursus in what was a speech concurring with the majority decision.

'The Welsh', he wrote,[88]

> are a nation – in the popular, though not the legal, sense – by reason of Offa's Dyke, by recollection of battles long ago and pride in the present valour of their regiments, because of musical gifts and religious dissent, because of fortitude in the face of economic adversity, because of satisfac-

84 Ibid. 85 For these facts see *Ealing London Borough Council v. Race Relations Board* [1972] AC 342. 86 Ibid., at 343–4. 87 See [1971] 1 QB 309. 88 [1972] AC at 364.

> tion of all Wales that Lloyd George became an architect of the welfare state and prime minister of victory.

Earlier in his speech, Lord Simon, in addressing himself to the identical problem, had sought to itemise the salient elements of Scottish-ness (and, in the process, was to refer to matters literary). 'Scotland', he wrote,[89]

> is not a nation in the eye of international law, but Scotsmen constitute a nation by reason of those most powerful elements in the creation of national spirit – tradition, folk memory, a sentiment of community.

And, he went on,

> The Scots are a nation because of Bannockburn and Flodden, Culloden and the pipes of Lucknow, because of Jenny Geddes and Flora Macdonald, because of frugal living and respect for learning, because of Robert Burns and Walter Scott.

It perhaps deserves to be noted that these words of Lord Simon were cited in a later Scots case where an Englishman presenting a sports programme on B.B.C. Scotland and replaced by a broadcaster with a Scots voice, like the Polish Mr Zesko, also claimed that he had been discriminated against.[90]

89 Ibid. 90 *BBC Scotland v. Souster*, 2001 SC 458. See especially the judgment of Lord Marnoch at 470.

CHAPTER 6

Nineteenth and twentieth centuries

SIR WALTER SCOTT
1771–1832

In the Middle Ages, Lord Anderson was to write in his learned disquisition on the inn in history (see above, p. 55 under BOCCACCIO), the traveller could look for necessary accommodation in three distinct directions.[1] One of these was 'the hospitality of those whose dwellings he passed' in the course of his journeyings. 'It will be remembered', he continued,[2]

> that in *Ivanhoe* the Templar, the Prior, the Jew, and the Palmer all obtained accommodation for the night from Cedric the Saxon.[3]

*

In the same disquisition, Lord Anderson mentions that in the Middle Ages the traveller might look to the monastery too for necessary accommodation.[4] 'Quentin Durward', he recalls,[5] 'and his charges and treacherous guide were entertained in a Franciscan monastery in the course of the journey from Plessis-lez-Tours to Liège'.[6]

*

In his account of the inn in history, Lord Anderson touches on one peculiarity of Scots law – the circumstance that a Scots Act of 1425, c.11 'authorised travellers with a large retinue to lodge with their friends, if they sent their horses and followers to the adjacent hostelry'.[7] There is a detail in the plot of *Rob Roy* that indicated that Scott had just this rule of law in mind. In the novel, Lord Anderson was to write,[8]

1 *Rothfield v. North British Ry. Co.*, 1920 SC 805 at 816. 2 Ibid. 3 *Ivanhoe*, chs. 3–6. 4 *Rothfield v. North British Ry. Co.*, 1920 SC 806 at 816. 5 Ibid. 6 *Quentin Durward*, ch. 16. 7 *Rothfield v. North British Ry. Co.*, 1920 SC 805 at 817. 8 Ibid.

when the convivial party of Highlanders attempted to exclude Bailie Nicol Jarvie from the inn at the Clachan of Aberfoyle, Frank Osbaldistone's position was absolutely sound in law when he said, 'I am yet to learn how three persons should be entitled to exclude all other travellers from the only place of shelter and refreshment for miles around.'[9]

*

In *Waverley*, too, in Lord Anderson's estimation, Scott may well have had in mind this self-same statute.[10] 'I have no doubt' that he had, Lord Anderson wrote, 'when in "Waverley"[11] he made the guests of Bradwardine leave their horses at Lucky Macleary's change house[12] in the village.'

*

Sir Walter Scott is listed along with Robert Burns as one of the architects of a sense of Scottish-ness in a speech of Lord Simon of Glaisdale in the House of Lords dealing with an allegation of discrimination in the administration of a housing list by a London borough council.[13] See above, pp 102–3 for the details of the case and for extracts from Lord Simon's speech.

CHARLES LAMB
1775–1834

In 1962, the Restrictive Practices Court in London upheld the Net Book Agreement 1957 as not being contrary to the public interest[14] – the critical test on the validity of such agreements under the Restrictive Trade Practices Act 1956.[15] In the judgment delivered by Mr Justice Buckley, the nature of 'the public' with whom and with whose interests as purchasers the court was necessarily concerned is the subject of some elucidation. Peccant bibliophiles recalled in an essay of Charles Lamb, appropriately enough in the circumstances, were worked into the image Mr Justice Buckley invited us to have of the consumers in question. 'It is … common ground', the judge declared,[16]

9 *Rob Roy*, ch. 28. 10 *Rothfield v. North British Ry. Co.*, 1920 SC 805 at 817. 11 *Waverley*, ch. 11. 12 A change-house was a small roadside inn. 13 *Ealing London Borough Council v. Race Relations Board* [1972] AC 342 at 364. 14 *In re Net Book Agreement, 1957* (1962) LR 3 RP 246, [1962] 1 WLR 1347. 15 4 & 5 Eliz. II, c. 68. 16 [1962] 1 WLR at 1375–6.

> that the public with whom we are concerned for the purposes of the subsection [s.21 (1) (b) of the Act] as consumers or users ... consists of individual retail buyers of books for their own reading, readers of books in public and institutional libraries, borrowers of books from all kinds of lending libraries and, no doubt, that class of borrowers also which Charles Lamb denounced as mutilators of collections, spoilers of the symmetry of shelves and creators of odd volumes,[17] the borrowers from private persons, as well as the recipients of books given as presents.

ALESSANDRO MANZONI
1785–1873

In *Ussher v. Ussher*,[18] in 1912, first Mr Justice Kenny and then the King's Bench Division (Lord O'Brien, CJ, Chief Baron Palles and Mr Justice Gibson) held that a marriage of two Roman Catholics in a ceremony conducted by a Roman Catholic priest, a Father Fahy, but in violation of the rules of the Council of Trent – only one witness was present – was nevertheless a valid marriage according to the common law in Ireland. Mr Justice Gibson, in his concurring judgment, frankly admitted that, out of deference to the arguments addressed to the court, he had considered a number of issues that only remotely touched the actual point for decision.[19] One such question he considered at some length was the precise function of the priest in the marriage ceremony. If the clergyman was there to verify and attest the consents of the parties to the marriage, that presupposed an active and willing co-operation on his part. Mr Justice Willes, the judge continued, had observed in *Beamish v. Beamish*[20] that there was no authority for the proposition that the parties could take advantage of the presence of a priest to marry one another in spite of him.[21] A central episode in Alessandro Manzoni's celebrated novel, *I promessi sposi* (1827), is recalled in Mr Justice Gibson's concluding observations on the point. 'Nor can I recall', the judge remarks,[22]

> any instance of an irregular marriage in which the minister did not purport to bind the union, or use some kind of rite, though no particular form may be essential. Such an incident as that described in Manzoni's *Promessi Sposi*, c. 8, referred to by counsel, where Renzo and Lucia attempt to say the

17 *Essays of Elia and Eliana* (1882): 'The two races of men', p. 39. 18 [1912] 2 IR 445. 19 At 528. 20 (1863) 9 HLC 274 at 325, 11 ER 735 at 755. 21 [1912] 2 IR at 515. 22 Ibid.

sacramental words before the surprised and frightened priest, Don Abbondio, represents a state of law quite unlike our Common Law.

The background to the extraordinary events that unfolded in Don Abbondio's study merits a word of explanation. The priest had been reciting his office on a walk near Lake Como one day in November 1628 when he was waylaid by two henchmen in the service of the local autocrat Don Rodrigo. Having confirmed that it was his intention on the morrow actually to marry Renzo Tramaglino and Lucia Mondella, Don Abbondio was then warned, at peril of his life, not to do anything of the sort. The priest's protest that parishioners availed of the services of the church in the matter in the same way as they went to a bank to draw money cut no ice at all with Don Rodrigo's men. The henchmen repeated their insistence that the wedding was not to take place – 'not tomorrow, and not any other time either'.

Don Abbondio then decides to postpone the ceremony, much, of course, to the consternation of Renzo, the prospective groom. A lawyer, Dottor Azzeccagarbugli,[23] and one Father Cristoforo, are consulted over what should now be done. It is, however, Agnese, Lucia's mother, who comes up with the solution it is agreed to put into practice – to catch Don Abbondio off guard and to contrive a marriage ceremony that would satisfy the requirements. All that was needed were two witnesses, a priest (even if the latter did not agree) and the exchange of sacramental declarations – by the groom, 'This is my wife', and by the bride, 'This is my husband'.[24] The scene was now set for the episode then described in chapter 8 of *I promessi sposi*, when Don Abbondio is burst in on in his own house.

GEORGE GORDON, LORD BYRON
1788–1824

Everson v. Board of Education of the Township of Ewing,[25] which came before the Supreme Court of the United States in 1946 and was decided in February 1947, was concerned with the constitutionality of a New Jersey statute which authorised the reimbursement to parents of money expended by them on the transportation of their children to and from certain categories of schools.[26] The specific problem concerned the payment in respect of the transportation of two

23 A made-up word = adroit weaver of tangles. 24 *I promessi sposi*, ch. 6. Cf. the views of the nineteenth-century German jurist, Professor Walter, repeated in *Beamish v. Beamish*, 9 HLC at 319–20, 11 ER at 753. 25 (1947) 330 U.S. 1. 26 New Jersey Laws, 1941, c. 191, p. 581.

children to a Catholic parochial school. The Supreme Court, by a majority, upheld the validity of the legislation, whilst conceding that it came perilously close to violating the separation of church and state under the United States Constitution.

Mr Justice Jackson and three other members of the court, chose to dissent. Mr Justice Jackson, for his part, found himself, he began,[27]

> contrary to first impressions, unable to join in this decision. I have a sympathy, though it is not ideological, with Catholic citizens who are compelled by law to pay taxes for public schools, and also feel constrained by conscience and discipline to support other schools for their own children. Such relief to them as this case involves is not in itself a serious burden to taxpayers and I had assumed it to be as little serious in principle.

But these first impressions, Mr Justice Jackson went on, had misled him. 'Study of the case,' he was to continue,[28]

> convinces me otherwise. The Court's opinion marshals every argument in favor of state aid and puts the case in its most favorable light, but much of its reasoning confirms my conclusions that there are no good grounds upon which to support the present legislation. In fact, the undertones of the opinion, advocating complete and uncompromising separation of Church from State, seem utterly discordant with its conclusion yielding support to their commingling in educational matters.

The coup de grâce is then delivered. 'The case which irresistibly comes to mind', Mr Justice Jackson concluded,[29]

> as the most fitting precedent is that of Julia who, according to Byron's reports, 'whispering "I will ne'er consent"' – consented.[30]

Julia, it deserves to be recalled, 'was married, charming, chaste, and twenty-three'.[31] It is in section 117 of Canto I of 'Don Juan' that we read of the abandonment of her original resolution to avoid seduction at the hands of Juan:[32]

> And Julia's voice was lost, except in sighs,
> Until too late for useful conversation;

27 330 U.S. at 18–19. 28 Ibid., at 19. 29 Ibid. 30 'Don Juan', Canto I, s. 117, line 936: Lord Byron, *The complete poetical works, vol. V; Don Juan*, ed. Jerome J. Mc Cann (Oxford, 1986), p. 46. 31 Ibid., Canto I, s. 59, line 472; Byron, *Complete poetical works: V*, p. 27. 32 Ibid., Canto I, s. 117: Byron, *Complete poetical works: V*, p. 46.

The tears were gushing from her gentle eyes,
I wish, indeed, they had not had occasion,
But who, alas! can love, and then be wise?
Not that remorse did not oppose temptation,
A little still she strove, and much repented,
And whispering 'I will ne'er consent'-consented.

THOMAS CARLYLE
1795–1881

In *In re O'Hara*,[33] the Irish Court of Appeal ordered the return of the 11-year-old Harriet O'Hara to her mother and stepfather. (For the background, see above, p. 101.) In his judgment in the Court of Appeal, Lord Justice Holmes composed a short panegyric in favour of 'the sympathy and help that spring from family affection'.[34] An allusion to the childhood of Robert Burns and the penury in which Burns was raised is followed by an equally telling reference to the childhood of Carlyle. Not far from Burns's country, Holmes wrote,[35]

> there is to be seen the birthplace of another famous Scotchman where, amidst mean surroundings, but learning the noblest lessons of love and duty, of self-sacrifice and piety, there grew up a family whose members, endowed with many and various gifts, had no possession more precious or more comforting than the strength of their kinship and their devotion to each other.

'Family affection', the judge continued, occupied an equally honoured place in local social practice. 'The light of genius', Holmes explained,[36]

> has made conspicuous the early days of Burns and Carlyle; but homes like theirs are to be found in rich abundance in every country. Indeed in none have family ties, knit together in poverty and suffering, borne richer fruit than in our own, as testified by the immense sums of money contributed by our emigrants for the help of parents and kinsfolk.

33 [1900] 2 IR 232. 34 At 257. 35 Ibid. 36 Ibid.

THOMAS HOOD
1799–1845

In *Hoare v. Robert Green Ltd* in 1907[37] the question posed was whether a room in a florists at Marylebone in London where wreaths were made up qualified as a 'workshop' for legal purposes. Protection of employees was accorded those working in a workshop under the terms of section 149 of the Factory and Workshop Act 1901. Where manual work was carried on at a place of employment counted as a workshop for purposes of the 1901 Act. In the King's Bench Division in London Mr Justice Phillimore had little difficulty in reaching the conclusion that the making up of wreaths qualified as manual labour. For good measure, the judge appended an apt literary allusion, to a celebrated poem in fact. 'Can anybody', the judge demanded rhetorically, 'who remembers Hood's "Song of the shirt" and the woman who stitched from morning to night think that she was not engaged in manual labour?'[38] The initial stanza of this poem of social protest, which first appeared in *Punch* on 16 December 1843, may here be given:

> With fingers weary and worn,
> With eyelids heavy and red,
> A woman sat, in unwomanly rags,
> Plying her needle and thread –
> Stitch! stitch! stitch!
> In poverty, hunger and dirt,
> And still with a voice of dolorous pitch
> She sang the 'Song of the Shirt'.[39]

ALEXANDRE DUMAS, PERE
1802–1870

In every century, Lord Anderson was to claim in his essay on the inn in history (see above, p. 55), the principal function of the hostelry had been to furnish rest and refreshment for the traveller.[40] In the case of inns in France, 'the writings ... of Dumas ... make this quite clear'.[41] So, too, did the writings of Spanish and Italian authors.

37 [1907] 2 KB 315. 38 Ibid., at 323. 39 For comment on this most celebrated of Hood's poems, see *Selected poems of Thomas Hood*, ed. with intro. and notes by John Clubbe (Cambridge, MA, 1970), pp 389–91. 40 *Rothfield v. North British Ry. Co.*, 1920 SC 805. 41 At 816.

BENJAMIN DISRAELI
1st earl of Beaconsfield, 1804–1881

In *Pratt v. Cook, Son & Co. (St Paul's) Ltd.* in 1938, the plaintiff brought an action under the Truck Act, 1831,[42] seeking a ruling that the contract for payment of part of his weekly wage was illegal, null and void.[43] Pratt earned 53*s.* in cash; in addition, 10*s.* was due him, represented by the cost of dinners and teas regularly served on the defendants' premises. The Truck Act in question provided that in all contracts for the performance by any artificer of any labour the wages were to be made payable in current coin of the realm and not otherwise. Pratt worked as a packer for the defendants, a firm of wholesale drapers, and was therefore covered by the legislation. Mr Justice Wrottesley held that the arrangements for the payment of Pratt – the meals instead of 10s. – violated the terms of the Truck Act and declared accordingly.[44] The Court of Appeal (Lords Justices Slesser, Finlay and Goddard) reversed, holding, in contradistinction to Wrottesley, that the employer could claim the benefit of a section in the Act of 1831, section 23, which provided that nothing in the Act was to extend to prevent the employer from furnishing to any artificer any victuals dressed or prepared under the employer's roof and consumed there by such artificer.[45]

In his concurring judgment, Lord Justice Goddard went out of his way to emphasise the role that the Truck Act had played in protecting the rights of workers. Disraeli the novelist is recalled in the process. 'The mischief against which the Act was aimed', Goddard remarks,[46]

> is well known; it has been described by many writers and by none more vividly than Disraeli in Book 3 of his novel 'Sybil'. Workmen were forced to take their wage partly and sometimes wholly in kind, or they were tied to the employer's shop, the tommy shop as it was called, for the purchase of necessaries; often wages were paid at such long intervals that the workman could only live by incurring credit with his employer for necessaries for which exorbitant prices were charged. The price was then deducted from his next wage, with the result that sometimes he got no money from year's end to year's end.

Disraeli's novel is loosely structured around the growing attachment between Charles Egremont, a member of the landlord class, and Sybil Gerard, the

42 1 & 2 Will. IV, c. 37. 43 As spelt out by s. 1. 44 [1938] 2 KB 51. 45 [1939] 1 KB 364. 46 At 382–3.

daughter of a militant Chartist leader. Disraeli's concern to pinpoint the contrast between the life of the rich and that of the poor finds him in Book 3 furnishing graphic images of the truck system – the arrangement under which, as Goddard explained in *Pratt's* case, the industrial worker was obliged to take his wages partly in kind and not 'in current coin of the realm'. A central image was that of the tommy-shop where truck tickets were exchangeable often for shoddy enough produce. A near riot at one such shop, Diggs's, is described in chapter 3 of Book 3, a prelude, it might be thought, to the actual destruction of the same shop in chapter 7 of Book 6. Truck itself is condemned by Nixon in the discussion of the topic among miners patronising the bar in the Rising Sun pub:[47]

> 'The question is', said Nixon, looking round with a magisterial air, 'what *is* wages? I say 'tayn't sugar, 'tayn't tea, 'tayn't bacon. I don't think 'tis candles; but of this I be sure, 'tayn't waistcoats.'

EDWARD FITZGERALD
1809–1883

Diarmuid O'Crowley, appointed a judge of the revolutionary Dáil courts, protested at their supersession by the Provisional Government in the summer of 1922, and was later to maintain he was appointed for life and ought therefore to have continued to be paid an annual salary of £750. This claim arose independently of his entitlement to a pension at the rate of £500 per annum which was paid to him after 1925.

When the new Fianna Fáil government which O'Crowley reckoned might have viewed his supposed entitlement to the larger sum with more sympathy came to power in 1932 and declined to accede to his wishes in the matter, O'Crowley resolved on legal proceedings. The case came before Mr Justice Johnston in the High Court in July 1934 who held against O'Crowley.[48] Since O'Crowley's office as a judge had been abolished by statute – the reference was to the Dáil Éireann Courts (Winding Up) Act 1923,[49] s.1(2) – and he could therefore no longer act in it, Johnston declared, he was no longer entitled to be paid any salary in respect of it, any existing contract having been discharged by impossibility of performance.

Mr Justice Johnston, in the final paragraph of his considered judgment,

47 Book 3, ch. 1. 48 *O'Crowley v. Minister for Justice and Minister for Finance* [1935] IR 536.
49 No. 36 of 1923.

dismissing O'Crowley's claim, labelled the claim itself, in all the circumstances, as 'ungracious'. An important review of O'Crowley's career, which concludes with a phrase from the Rubáiyát, indicates why exactly the judge had reached such a verdict:[50]

> Mr O'Crowley has been treated not only justly but even generously by his country ... He retired in early middle age from his work in the Customs and Excise of the former Government to live for the rest of his life on his savings and a small pension of nearly £100 a year. He was then called to the Bar and after a very limited experience of four years he was appointed to a judicial office at a salary of £750. He served for barely two years in that office and he is then granted a further pension of £500 a year. In my opinion he has nothing to complain of. Most of the young men who, risking everything, went out into the wilderness in 1919 would, I feel sure, have been content to say: 'And wilderness were Paradise enow'.[51]

*

A complete verse from Edward Fitzgerald's rendition of Omar Khayyám was to be incorporated by Mr Justice Lynch into his judgment for the Irish Supreme Court in *Carna Foods Ltd. v. Eagle Star Insurance Co. (Ireland) Ltd.*[52] The defendant insurance company announced that they were cancelling or not renewing five insurance policies covering fire, employer's liability and public liability standing in the name of the plaintiff company and of its managing director. No reasons were given, which furnished the gravamen of the plaintiffs' complaint against their insurers. A major plank in the plaintiffs' case was the novel contention that there could be implied into all insurance policies a term to the effect that if cover was ever cancelled or withdrawn the insurer had to furnish reasons for this course of action. In the High Court action, Mr Justice McCracken refused to accept so radical a contention.[53] In the Supreme Court Mr Justice Lynch was, if anything, even more forthright. It was very likely – so ran the argument – that if at the pre-contract stage the plaintiffs had sought such a term to be included in the insurance contract the insurers would not have contracted with the plaintiffs at all.[54]

50 [1935] IR at 550. 51 Edward Fitzgerald, *Rubáiyát of Omar Khayyám*, 1st ed. (London, 1859), xi; 4th ed. (London, 1879), xii. In the 1st ed. the line in Fitzgerald's translation reads: 'And Wilderness is Paradise enow'. And in the 4th: 'Oh, Wilderness were Paradise enow'. Plainly Mr Justice Johnston chose to conflate the two versions. See, conveniently, *The Rubáiyát of Omar Khayyám*, ed. A.J. Arberry (London, 1949), p. 125. 52 [1997] 2 IR 193. 53 *Carna Foods Ltd. v. Eagle Star Insurance Co. (Ireland) Ltd.* [1995] 1 IR 526. 54 [1997] 2 IR at 200.

A further claim advanced on behalf of the plaintiffs was that the defendant, in addition to stating reasons, should be under an implied obligation to put the plaintiffs back into the same position that they enjoyed regarding the obtaining of insurance cover before they entered into their contracts of insurance with Eagle Star. Mr Justice Lynch was again unimpressed.[55] It was to be in the manner of expressing his disbelief at this allied contention that he found the occasion for quoting from Omar Khayyám. This contention on the part of the plaintiffs, he asserted,[56]

> is an impossibility. The fact is that the plaintiffs did contract with the defendant as their insurers and that the defendant cancelled two of the policies and declined to renew the other three policies and that will always be the position. One recalls the often quoted lines of the poet Edward Fitzgerald:[57]
>
> The moving finger writes; and having writ,
> moves on: nor all thy piety nor wit
> shall lure it back to cancel half a line,
> nor all thy tears wash out a word of it.

ALFRED LORD TENNYSON
1809–1892

John Coyle, a carpenter by trade, was engaged by his firm in the construction of a signal-box for the Great Northern Railway Co. at their railway station in Drogheda. The tools used by Mr Coyle and his fellow employees were kept in a tool-box placed at the opposite side of the railway line. Early in the morning of 15 April 1886 Coyle went to the tool-box to fetch his implements. Crossing back to the other side of the railway line, Coyle was knocked down and killed. An engine was shunting carriages down the line to make up the up-luggage train for Dublin and this was when Coyle was killed. It was a fine, clear morning and daylight. Coyle had his eyesight and was not deaf.

Though the jury at the hearing of an action brought by Coyle's widow under Lord Campbell's Act found in favour of the plaintiff and awarded her £250 damages, the trial judge, Mr Justice Lawson, specifically left open the prospect of the defendants moving to have the verdict and judgment entered in their

55 At 202. 56 Ibid. 57 Edward Fitzgerald, *Rubáiyát of Omar Khayyám*, 1st ed. (London, 1859), li.

favour. The Great Northern Railway Co. accordingly moved for a conditional order to secure precisely that. The case thus arrived in the Exchequer Division (Chief Baron Palles and Baron Dowse), where the court, reviewing everything that transpired, ruled in favour of the defendants. Mrs Coyle was thus denied the fruits of her earlier victory.[58]

The time of the Exchequer Division was taken up in reexamining the approach of the trial judge to handling the allegation of negligence against the railway company and the counter-allegation of contributory negligence against Coyle. Linked to this was the initial question of whether the case should have been withdrawn from the jury on the grounds that there was no evidence of negligence on the part of the defendants. Reviewing the authorities,[59] Chief Baron Palles concluded that the case ought not to have been left to the jury. For his part, Baron Dowse agreed but, at the outset of his judgment he alluded to confusion in the legal authorities and the challenge that these, quite independently, presented. He was to quote Tennyson – the few well-known lines from 'Aylmer's Field'.[60]

'This case', the baron began,[61] 'affords an apt illustration of the truth contained in the Laureate's lines, when he spoke of:

> ... the lawless science of our law –
> That codeless myriad of precedent,
> That wilderness of single instances.

'Here', he went on,

> we have judges differing from one another, and, what is worse and more confusing, sometimes differing from themselves. Our duty is to endeavour to extract a principle from these 'single instances', and this duty has been discharged by the Chief Baron in this case.

*

Boyle v. Lee and Goyns in 1991[62] witnessed another attempt by the Irish Supreme Court to clarify the solution to problems in Irish conveyancing generated by the requirement introduced by the Statute of Frauds in 1695[63] that there

58 *Coyle v. Great Northern Railway Co.* (1887) 20 LR Ir 409. 59 And, in particular, the difficult case of *Slattery v. Dublin, Wicklow and Wexford Railway Co.* (1874) IR 8 CL 531; (1876) IR 10 CL 256; (1878) 3 App. Cas. 1155. 60 *The works of Alfred Lord Tennyson, poet laureate* (London, 1911), p. 142 at p. 149. 61 20 LR Ir at 429. 62 [1992] ILRM 65. 63 7 Will. III, c. 7, s. 2.

must always exist a sufficient note or memorandum of the agreement buttressing any actual transaction. In the circumstances of the case, the decision that prevailed was to the effect that the essential terms of the envisaged contract had not been finalised and that therefore there was no compliance with the requirements of the Statute of Frauds.

In a paragraph in his judgment designed, one surmises, to furnish the context in which best to regard the final decision, Mr Justice McCarthy manages to intrude a well-known phrase of Tennyson's. 'It is a feature of property transactions in Ireland', the judge avers,[64]

> that they are often made with a minimum of formality, the circumstances, including the venue, of such bargains not being always conducive to the 'dusty purlieus of the law'.[65]

*

In *Keane v. An Bord Pleanála* in 1996[66] the Supreme Court by a majority held that the Commissioners of Irish Lights had no power under legislation of 1894 to construct at a site in Co. Clare a 750 feet tall mast forming part of a Loran-C navigational system. (This is a position-fixing system based on the transmission and reception of low frequency electro-magnetic waves or pulses.) Only if the court agreed that the system constituted a 'lighthouse', a 'buoy' or a 'beacon' within the contemplation of the Merchant Shipping Act 1894,[67] could the erection of the mast by the commissioners be adjudged lawful. The majority of the Supreme Court held it could not. Two judges, Mr Justice O'Flaherty and Mrs Justice Denham dissented, holding that it could.

Tennyson comes to the aid of Mr Justice O'Flaherty in deciding that the word 'beacon' could be given an expanded definition. 'It is clear', he wrote,[68]

> that in Britain, by virtue of the Merchant Shipping Act, 1979, there is given to the relevant government minister an express power to extend the definition of 'beacon' to take account of modern development but just because the Oireachtas has not done likewise does not absolve the courts from the duty of deciding whether the old Act will pass muster to encompass this new device. I hold that it is asking too much of the legislature to be on the alert to amend old legislation to take account of every new development. In the

64 [1992] ILRM at 78. 65 Tennyson, 'In memoriam', lxxxix. 66 [1997] 1 IR 184. 67 57 & 58 Vict., c. 60. 68 [1997] 1 IR at 219.

circumstances, I have no difficulty in holding that the word 'beacon' should include radio beacons, including beacons erected for the purposes of marine navigation. Though more sophisticated, and with a longer [r]each, I hold this mast serves essentially the same purpose as did the beacon in Tennyson's lines:

> Henceforth, wherever thou may'st roam
> My blessing, like a line of light,
> Is on the waters day and night,
> And like a beacon guards thee home.[69]

*

In *Gray v. Gee* in 1923[70] (see below, p. 126) Mr Justice Darling heard a case in which a married woman sued another woman for enticing away her husband. The special jury, who sat with Mr Justice Darling, found in favour of the other woman, and the action was dismissed with costs.[71]

Mr Justice Darling was faced with a preliminary objection raised by the defendant. Mr Clements, who appeared for the latter, agreed that whilst a husband could maintain such an action, a wife could not. Counsel's argument had been that there was a fundamental difference between the rights of a husband and the rights of a wife, and these went back to the time when the wife was the property of her husband, who owned her just as he did any other chattel.[72] The judge, in rehearsing Mr Clements' argument, then quoted from Tennyson's 'Locksley Hall':[73]

> He will hold thee, when his passion shall have spent its novel force
> Something better than his dog, a little dearer than his horse.

Mr Justice Darling, however, while conceding that such matters helped to explain why no such action on the part of a wife had been brought before, held that legal changes, witnessed principally by the Married Women's Property Act 1882,[74] had radically altered the situation.

The preliminary objection to the hearing of the case was thus ruled to be bad.[75]

'Locksley Hall' is a tale of the love of cousins, of family estrangement and of

69 Tennyson, 'In memoriam', xvii. 70 (1923) 39 Times LR 429. 71 Ibid., at 431. 72 39 Times LR at 431. 73 Alfred Tennyson, *Poems*, new ed. (London, 1976), p.267 at p. 270. 74 45 & 46 Vict., c. 75. 75 39 Times LR 431.

the narrator's loss of his cousin Amy who married someone else and, in the process, suffered rather more than *capitis diminutio*. As the poem expresses it:[76]

> Is it well to wish thee happy? – having known me – to decline
> On a range of lower feelings and a narrower heart than mine!
> Yet it shall be: thou shalt lower to his level day by day,
> What is fine within thee growing coarse to sympathize with clay.
> As the husband is, the wife is: thou art mated with a clown,
> And the grossness of his nature will have weight to drag thee down.

There then follow the two lines quoted by Mr Justice Darling in *Gray v. Gee*.

'Locksley Hall' was composed by Tennyson at some point in the 1830's.[77] In 1886 he produced a sequel, 'Sixty years after', when the passionate narrator of the earlier poem, now an old man of 80, revisits the past, his agonies over cousin Amy, long dead in childbirth, and his hatred of her husband, the 'clown' of 'Locksley Hall,' dead now too. In 'Sixty years after,' Tennyson also berates his own failures in life, his personal tragedies, and, like Dickens and Trollope in their later novels, 'the growth of a soulless commercialism'.[78]

CHARLES DICKENS
1812–1870

In his extended essay on the inn in history (for the background to which see above, p. 55), Lord Anderson was to draw attention to a subsidiary function that came to be established in modern times, in the case at least of inns situated in populous places: 'They were used as meeting places by local residents who were socially inclined.'[79] An illustration from Dickens is appended:

> In *Barnaby Rudge* the parish clerk and his cronies met in the evenings at 'The Maypole' to drink their ale and smoke churchwarden pipes.[80]

'The Maypole' is introduced to the reader at the outset of the novel. 'In the year 1775', Dickens tells us,[81]

> there stood upon the borders of Epping Forest, at a distance of about twelve miles from London … a house of public entertainment called the

76 Tennyson, *Poems*, at p. 270. 77 Charles Tennyson, *Alfred Tennyson* (New York, 1949), pp 193–94. 78 Ibid., p. 491. 79 *Rothfield v. North British Ry. Co.*, 1920 SC 805 at 817. 80 Scenes at 'The Maypole' regularly punctuate the plot in *Barnaby Rudge*. 81 *Barnaby Rudge*, ch. 1.

> Maypole; which fact was demonstrated to all such travellers as could neither read nor write (and at that time a vast number both of travellers and stay-at-homes were in this condition) by the emblem reared on the roadside over against the house, which, if not of those goodly proportions that Maypoles were wont to present in olden times, was a fair young ash, thirty feet in height, and straight as any arrow that ever English yeoman drew.

*

On 16 January 1926, Dr Henry McKeogh, the local medical officer of health for a dispensary district on the Tipperary/Clare border, wrote to the Department of Local Government and Public Health to complain about a local midwife.

> I beg to intimate to you that Mrs Nolan, midwife, Ballina, Killaloe (Portroe Dispensary District) shows remarkable want of cleanliness when conducting her cases. There were at least two cases of puerperal fever during the past eight months in the above district.[82]

The contents of the letter became known to Mrs Nolan, and the upshot was the libel case of *Nolan v. McKeogh*. Mrs Nolan lost, the doctor's communication being held to be privileged. But more in fact was to follow, for Mrs Nolan consulted a solicitor in Limerick, Mr Hugh O'Brien Moran, who, arguing he was entitled to stand in the shoes of Mrs Nolan, in a letter, made counter-allegations against Dr McKeogh. Mrs Nolan, the solicitor was to write, 'will be able to prove when the time comes that there was greater reason for complaint against Dr McKeogh in his treatment of patients than there was against her'. This serious accusation grounded a second libel action, of the doctor against the solicitor.[83] In the High Court, Mr Justice Hanna held that the solicitor's accusation against Dr McKeogh raised an independent and extraneous matter and no privilege could thereby attach to it. The doctor accordingly was entitled to a verdict in his favour.

Inevitably, perhaps, attempts were made to draw some kind of portrait of Mrs – or, if you like, Nurse – Nolan. This issue of characterisation was revisited by Mr Justice Hanna, recalling, in the process, one of Dickens's more celebrated, if hardly estimable, protagonists from *Martin Chuzzlewit*. Nurse Nolan, the judge was to write, 'was compared with that famous nurse of fiction, Sairey Gamp'.[84]

82 Reproduced, [1927] IR at 350 and 352. 83 *McKeogh v. O'Brien Moran* [1927] IR 348. 84 [1927] IR at 352.

He added that, just as in Dickens's novel, 'Mrs Harris was alleged to say "Bring in Sairey", I think it is clear that in recent years Nurse Nolan would recommend Dr Holmes [a rival doctor to Dr McKeogh] to her patients'.[85] It is in chapter 19 of *Chuzzlewit* that we first make the acquaintance of Mrs Gamp. She lodged in High Holborn in London, we are told, 'at a bird-fancier's, next door but one to the celebrated mutton-pie shop, and directly opposite to the original cat's meat warehouse'. Hardly more salubrious than the address was the lady herself, for, as Dickens advises us, on more than one occasion, Mrs Gamp had a craving for alcohol; the whiff of the stuff would accompany her on most of her perambulations. When she appears in chapter 25, for instance, the appearance brought with it 'a peculiar fragrance ... borne upon the breeze, as if a passing fairy had hiccoughed, and had previously been to a wine-vaults'. Nurse Nolan, on the other hand, as Mr Justice Hanna was to be at some pains to point out, despite any other allegations that might have been laid against her, at least 'had none of [Mrs Gamp's] bibulous habits'.[86]

Readers familiar with developments that occur in *Martin Chuzzlewit* will be aware naturally of one point of comparison between our two midwives, the one fictional and the other from Killaloe. Mrs Gamp had a falling-out with Betsey Prig over the redoubtable Mrs Harris. Nurse Nolan, too, it would appear, had not been able to remain on the right side of all those who mattered in her neck of the woods.

*

In Lord Anderson's excursus devoted to the inn in history, to which reference has already been made (see above, *Barnaby Rudge*, p. 118 and also p. 55) the judge makes the point that

> with the establishment of stage-coaches in later times, and increase in the numbers of the travelling public, the discharge of his primary function in accommodating travellers became more manifestly the main business of the innkeeper.[87]

Pickwick Papers furnished one very obvious example:

> It will be remembered that Mr Pickwick and his friends were travellers *in itinere* from Birmingham to London when they put up for the night at

85 Ibid. 86 Ibid. 87 *Rothfield v. North British Ry. Co.*, 1920 SC 805 at 817.

> 'The Saracen's Head', Towcester,[88] and witnessed the historic combat between the rival journalists of Eatanswill.[89]

The host at the Saracen's Head, Dickens tells us – if Lord Anderson does not – chose to venture, for the benefit of the Pickwickians,

> a variety of dismal conjectures regarding the state of the roads, the doubt of fresh horses being to be had at the next stage, the dead certainty of its raining all night, the equally mortal certainty of its clearing up in the morning, and other topics of inducement familiar to innkeepers.[90]

*

Chapter 34 of *The Pickwick Papers*, 'Is wholly devoted to a full and faithful Report of the memorable Trial of Bardell against Pickwick', features at the outset the swearing in before an irascible Mr Justice Stareleigh of the jury destined to pronounce on this celebrated breach of promise action. Matters do not proceed smoothly, much to the annoyance of the presiding judge, when one of the putative jurors applies to be excused. This is Thomas Groffin, a chemist, who has not been able to employ an assistant to stand in for him at the pharmacy should his attendance elsewhere be required. When the judge disallows the application, Groffin protests, claiming that if he is indeed obliged to serve on the jury, 'Then there'll be murder before this trial's over'. An explanation is immediately volunteered after Groffin is sworn:

> 'I merely wanted to observe, my Lord', said the chemist, taking his seat with great deliberation, 'that I've left nobody but an errand-boy in my shop. He is a very nice boy, my Lord, but he is not acquainted with drugs; and I know that the prevailing impression in his mind is, that Epsom salts means oxalic acid; and syrup of senna, laudanum. That's all, my Lord'. With this, the tall chemist composed himself into a comfortable attitude, and, assuming a pleasant expression of countenance, appeared to have prepared himself for the worst.

The Queen v. Pharmaceutical Society which came before the Irish Queen's Bench Division in 1896[91] concerned an apparent contradiction in the criteria

88 *Pickwick Papers*, ch. 51. 89 Ibid. On the rivalry between the journalists of the *Eatanswill Gazette* and the *Eatanswill Independent*, see, too, *Pickwick Papers*, ch. 13, entitled 'Some account of Eatanswill; of the state of parties therein, and of the election of a member to serve in Parliament for that ancient, loyal, and patriotic borough'. 90 *Pickwick Papers*, ch. 51. 91 [1896] 2 IR 368.

for qualification as a dispensing chemist as between a statutory provision contained in the Pharmacy (Ireland) Act of 1875[92] and a regulation adopted by the Pharmaceutical Society of Ireland established under the self-same Act and touching on the same question.

Having resolved the issue in question, Mr Justice Holmes, for his part, added a few words which he labelled as 'not strictly judicial'.[93] He was certain that the Council of the Pharmaceutical Society had acted *bona fide*. 'I am sure', he observed, 'that they are sincerely anxious to uphold the standard of a profession which is of great value to the country.' The allusion to Dickens, entirely predictable in the circumstances, then followed:[94]

> The time has gone by for leaving the public to the mercy of the chemist's errand-boy of 'Pickwick', with his confused ideas about oxalic acid and Epsom salts, laudanum and syrup of senna.

*

In her will of September 1937 Charlotte Frances Shaw, the wife of George Bernard Shaw, bequeathed the residue of her estate on the following trusts:

> The making of grants contributions and payments to any foundation corporate body institution association or fund ... having for its object the bringing of the masterpieces of fine art within the reach of the people of Ireland of all classes in their own country ... The teaching promotion and encouragement in Ireland of self control, elocution, oratory, deportment, the arts of personal contact, of social intercourse, and the other arts of public, private, professional and business life.

In 1951 in the English Chancery Division Mr Justice Vaisey held that these trusts were wholly educational in character and, this being so, no evidence was required to demonstrate benefit to the community.[95] Mrs Shaw's employment in these arrangements of the word 'deportment' did cause Mr Justice Vaisey to pause momentarily. In dismissing any objection that might be thought thereby to have arisen, the judge included an entirely appropriate reference to one of Charles Dickens's more exotic characters. In a critical clause in the will, Mr Justice Vaisey argued,[96]

92 38 & 39 Vict., c. 57. 93 [1896] 2 IR at 390. 94 Ibid. 95 *In re Shaw's Will Trusts* [1952] Ch. 163. The fate of her husband's will might be compared: see below, p. 132. 96 [1952] Ch. at 168.

> there are obviously many ways in which the trust income could be usefully applied, within the terms there laid down, and it is not, in my view, admissible to test the matter by presupposing perverse and unreasonable methods of applying it, as, for example, the method of devoting it entirely to the teaching and encouragement of 'deportment', though, after all, that word means nothing except 'manners', however much its significance may have been debased by its connexion with the character of Mr Turveydrop in *Bleak House*, in which the word is usually printed with a capital 'D'.

Dickens's introduction of this remarkable creature merits being rehearsed.[97] '"Old Mr Turveydrop" – there was a young Mr Turveydrop, "Prince", christened thus in remembrance of the Prince Regent' ('Old Mr Turveydrop adored the Prince Regent on account of his Deportment') –

> was a fat old gentleman with a false complexion, false teeth, false whiskers, and a wig. He had a fur collar, and he had a padded breast to his coat, which only wanted a star or a broad blue ribbon to be complete. He was pinched in, and swelled out, and got up, and strapped down, as much as he could possibly bear. He had such a neckcloth on (puffing his very eyes out of their natural shape), and his chin and even his ears so sunk into it, that it seemed as though he must inevitably double up, if it were cast loose. He had, under his arm, a hat of great size and weight, shelving downward from the crown to the brim; and in his hand a pair of white gloves, with which he flapped it, as he stood poised on one leg, in a high-shouldered, round-elbowed state of elegance not to be surpassed. He had a cane, he had an eye-glass, he had a snuff-box, he had rings, he had wristbands, he had everything but any touch of nature; he was not like youth, he was not like age, he was like nothing in the world but a model of Deportment.

*

In chapter 51 of *Oliver Twist* we find Mr Brownlow about to resolve the riddle of Oliver's ancestry. Proof had come to light that Mrs Bumble, the wife of the beadle at the workhouse, Bumble, had filched a gold locket and ring from Oliver's mother who had died soon after giving birth to Oliver. Both the locket and the ring were later to be pawned. Their importance lay in the circumstance that they were proof of Oliver's ancestry. Presented with this uncomfortable

97 *Bleak House*, ch. 14, appropriately enough entitled 'Deportment'.

intelligence which was bound to cause his loss of employment, Bumble struck out, 'It was all Mrs Bumble,' he burst forth, first having looked around, Dickens tells us, to ascertain that his partner had left the room. 'She *would* do it.'

Brownlow knew his law and, in particular, doctrine on so-called marital coercion in the criminal law.[98] This prompted his rebuff to Bumble. 'That is no excuse,' Brownlow was to reply:

> You were present on the occasion of the destruction of these trinkets, and indeed are the more guilty of the two, in the eye of the law; for the law supposes that your wife acts under your direction.

At this, Bumble exploded, uttering in the process his celebrated *dictum*, as it came to be known, on law. Squeezing his hat emphatically in both hands, Bumble produced his much-quoted retort:

> If the law supposes that, the law is a ass – a idiot. If that's the eye of the law, the law is a bachelor; and the worst I wish the law is, that his eye may be opened by experience – by experience.

Barrett v. Irvine,[99] the Roscarberry foxhounds affair to which allusion has earlier been made in the Introduction, furnishes one instance – there may naturally be a number of others – where a serving judge has referred to Bumble's *dictum* in the course of a reported judgment. The judge in this case, one featuring 'the gallant attempt to establish a somewhat Irish agency in an environment of infancy and fox-hunting',[1] was the then Irish lord chief justice, Lord O'Brien of Kilfenora. (Kilfenora is in Co. Clare on the edge of the Burren.) 'If this case is deemed worthy of a place in our law books,' Lord O'Brien began,[2]

> or is made the subject of story in any metropolitan or local magazine, it may be well intituled 'The Enfant Gâté of Roscarberry'.[3] A fond mother paid some money – the price of horses which her son, a spoilt boy had bought, and it is argued that she thereby held him out to the world as, and constituted him, her general agent to buy horses on her credit to any extent his juvenile fancy might suggest. That, in fact, if another Waterloo was to be fought in defence of the liberties of Europe, this impulsive youth might

98 The doctrine has been abandoned in the modern law, in Ireland the conclusion being founded on an interpretation of the Constitution: *The State (D.P.P.) v. Walsh and Connelly* [1981] IR 412; see at 449. 99 [1907] 2 IR 462. 1 R.E. Megarry, *Miscellany-at-law* (London, 1955), p. 211. 2 [1907] 2 IR at 467. 3 i.e. 'The spoilt child of R'. Roscarberry is situated in west Co. Cork.

> horse, at her expense, a brigade of the Greys, Inniskillings, and 1st Royals, to add another page to the history of chivalry.

After that, the predictable *coup de grâce* followed. 'If the law permits this,' Lord O'Brien continued,[4]

> the man in the street, to whom I have so often referred as the embodiment of common sense, may well regard Mr Bumble's famous *dictum* not merely as historical, but true.

Marital coercion partly survives as a defence in England and Wales. Section 47 of the Criminal Justice Act 1925[5] represents the present law there. It provides as follows:

> Any presumption of law that an offence committed by a wife in the presence of her husband is committed under the coercion of the husband is hereby abolished, but on a charge against a wife for any offence other than treason or murder, it shall be a good defence to prove that the offence was committed in the presence of, and under the coercion of, the husband.

Jefferson's examination of modern English discussion of section 47[6] touches on problems generated by the polygamous wife and the woman who might mistakenly believe she is indeed married. He also quotes the conclusion of an American court from as long ago as 1881[7] to the effect that coercion was the 'relic of a belief in the ignorance and pusillanimity of women'.

ROBERT BROWNING
1812–1889

In 1918 one Marks Feigenbaum was convicted of the offences of having incited some boys to steal sacks of fodder, and of having received the fodder knowing it to have been stolen. He was sentenced to four years' penal servitude. In the circumstances, the boys were, however, Feigenbaum's accomplices and when the case reached the Court of Criminal Appeal the following year[8] Mr Justice Darling was at pains to stress the obligations of a trial judge when directing a

4 [1907] 2 IR at 67. 5 15 & 16 Geo. V, c. 86. 6 Michael Jefferson, *Criminal law*, 7th ed. (Harlow, 2006), pp 248–9. 7 *U.S. v. de Quilfeldt* (1881) 5F. 276. 8 *R. v. Marks Feigenbaum* [1919] 1 KB 431.

jury on the evidence of accomplices.[9] Robert Browning was to be quoted where the judge stressed the subtleties that existed in the relevant legal rules. 'It has been laid down in many cases', the judge was to observe,[10]

> that the judge ought not to leave the case to the jury without warning them firmly that the evidence of an accomplice must always be regarded with grave suspicion, and that they ought not to convict unless the evidence of the accomplice is corroborated; further, he ought to point out to the jury what corroborative evidence there is, if any, or if, in his opinion, there is no corroborative evidence, he should tell the jury so.

'Practically', the judge continued,[11]

> this differs little from saying that a judge may direct an acquittal if there is indeed no corroboration of the accomplice's evidence, but a difference does exist, though it may be very slight. In the words of Browning:
>
> 'Oh the little more, and how much it is!
> And the little less, and what worlds away.'[12]

MATTHEW ARNOLD
1822–1888

In *Gray* v. *Gee* in 1923,[13] as we have already recalled (above, p. 117), Mr Justice Darling and a special jury had to decide whether a wife could successfully sue another woman for enticing away her husband. In theory, the judge advised, she could, even if the result in the case was that the other woman, a Miss Gee, emerged triumphant from the court, the jury having returned a verdict in her favour.

The theoretical difficulty addressed by Mr Justice Darling found him in expansive mood, scarcely unexpected in light of the judge's known talents and interests. 'That a woman', he had begun,[14]

> could seduce a man he did not doubt; it had been the theme of many poets, and people were accustomed in the old days to make use of love philtres to seduce the affections of other people. Such stories were common at the

9 At 433–4. 10 At 433. 11 Ibid. 12 'By the Fire-Side', xxxix, lines 1–2. 13 (1923) 39 Times LR 429. 14 39 Times LR at 431.

> time of the Renaissance. There had been many women who thought that they could gain the affection of men by getting them to drink some potion.

The judge then proceeded to instance the description of such a potion included in Matthew Arnold's well-known poem. 'It was described in the lines from "Tristram and Iseult"':[15]

> ... that spiced magic draught,
> Which since then for ever rolls
> Through their blood, and binds their souls,
> Working love, but working teen.

The passage comes in Arnold's poem when the dying Tristram anticipates the arrival of the second Iseult in his life – Iseult of Brittany – but ponders the whereabouts of the first Iseult – Iseult of Ireland:[16]

> Iseult of Brittany? – but where
> Is that other Iseult fair,
> That proud, first Iseult, Cornwall's queen?
> She, whom Tristrams's ship of yore,
> From Ireland to Cornwall bore,
> To Tyntagel, to the side
> Of King Marc, to be his bride?
> She who, as they voyaged, quaff'd
> With Tristram that spiced magic draught.

In the belief that it was wine, Tristram and Iseult no. 1 had drunk the potion that united them in everlasting love. Iseult who prepared the potion had intended it for her future husband King Marc. The joint mistake of Tristram and Iseult had the inevitable consequences.[17]

15 Matthew Arnold, *Poems* (London, 1890), at p. 201. 16 Ibid. 17 For a re-examination of the suspicions of King Marc of the true state of affairs later as between Queen Iseult (Isolt) and Tristram (Tristan) and of his endeavours to gather evidence, in other versions of the story, see Roger D. Groot, 'Isolt's trial and ordeal: a legal-historical analysis' in Paul Brand, Kevin Costello and W.N. Osborough (ed.), *Adventures of the law: Proceedings of the 16th British Legal History Conference, Dublin, 2003* (Dublin, 2005), p. 1.

LEWIS CARROLL

Charles Lutwidge Dodgson, 1832–1898

In Britain regulation 18B of the Defence (General) Regulations 1939 provided:

> If the Secretary of State has reasonable cause to believe any person to be of hostile origin or associations or to have been recently concerned in acts prejudicial to the public safety or the defence of the realm or in the preparation or instigation of such acts and that by reason thereof it is necessary to exercise control over him, he may make an order against that person directing that he be detained.

One Robert William Liversidge was ordered to be detained[18] under this regulation by Sir John Anderson, the then Home Secretary. Liversidge sued for false imprisonment but met with no success, the House of Lords who were eventually seized of the case, holding, by a majority, that a court of law could not inquire whether the Home Secretary had in fact reasonable grounds for his belief.[19] In a celebrated dissent, Lord Atkin protested against what he regarded as 'a strained interpretation put on words with the effect of giving an uncontrolled power of imprisonment to the minister'.[20] He had earlier felt compelled to observe that in the course of the hearing in the Lords he had listened 'to arguments which might have been addressed acceptably to the Court of King's Bench in the time of Charles I'.[21]

Warming to his theme, he was to turn to a passage in the dialogue between Humpty Dumpty and Alice in *Through the looking-glass* to point up the semantic error being perpetrated and which had left his judicial brethren quite unfazed. 'I know of only one authority', Lord Atkin continued,[22] 'which might justify the suggested method of construction [of regulation 18B]':

> 'When I use a word', Humpty Dumpty said in rather a scornful tone, 'it means just what I choose it to mean – neither more nor less.'
> 'The question is', said Alice, 'whether you *can* make words mean so many different things.'
> 'The question is', said Humpty Dumpty, 'which is to be Master – that's all.'[23]

18 On 26 May 1940. 19 *Liversidge v. Anderson* [1942] AC 206. 20 [1942] AC at 244. 21 Ibid. 22 [1942] AC at 245. 23 *Through the looking-glass and what Alice found there*, ch. 6.

And Lord Atkin deduced from this excursus of his the obvious – or what he at least viewed as the obvious – corollary. 'After all this long discussion', he concluded,[24]

> the question is whether the words 'If a man has' can mean 'If a man thinks he has'. I am of opinion that they cannot, and that the case should be decided accordingly.

SIR WILLIAM SCHWENK GILBERT
1836–1911

In *Thomas v. The King* in 1937, the High Court of Australia was confronted with a problem in the law of bigamy.[25] Did the man's honest and reasonable, though mistaken, belief that a prior marriage of the woman he had first married had not been dissolved (the decree nisi not having been made absolute) and that this former marriage of his was invalid entail that he was lawfully entitled to go through the ceremony of marriage in respect of which the charge of bigamy had been laid? By a majority of 3–2 the court held that such a belief did constitute a defence. The initial legislation in the case – a section in the Victorian Crimes Act 1928[26] – did not envisage such circumstances and had nothing to say to them, but standard principles of interpretation which would interpose a requirement of mens rea, were on hand to be called in aid. 'When a statute was introduced into our criminal code', Mr Justice Dixon was to remark,

> it should be understood prima facie to intend the offence to take its place in a coherent general system and to be governed by the established principles of criminal responsibility.[27]

Such an approach – it can be termed the liberal one – Mr Justice Dixon had observed earlier in his judgment had in fact been mocked by the Mikado.[28] This was in his answer to the assurance of Koko and his companions that they had no idea and knew nothing about it and were not there:[29]

> That's the pathetic part of it. Unfortunately the fool of an Act says 'compassing the death of the heir-apparent'. There's not a word about mistake, or not knowing, or having no notion, or not being there. There

24 See further, R.F.V. Heuston, 'Liversidge *v.* Anderson in retrospect', *Law Quarterly Review*, lxxxvi (1970), 33. 25 (1937) 59 CLR 279. 26 No. 3664. 27 59 CLR at 304. 28 59 CLR at 303–4. 29 *The Mikado*, act II.

should be of course; but there isn't. That's the slovenly way in which these Acts are always drawn.

ANATOLE FRANCE
Jacques-Anatole-François Thibault, 1844–1924

Anatole France's short story *Crainquebille*[30] received rather more than a passing mention in the charge of Mr Justice Hanna to a jury in the personal injuries action of *Walsh v. Dublin United Tramways Co.* heard in 1931.[31] The issue arose of the credibility and indeed the reliability of police evidence in the case. In France's story Jerome Crainquebille was wrongly convicted of insulting a policeman, imprisoned for a fortnight and fined 50 francs. A costermonger by profession, his erstwhile clientele abandoned him after his release from prison, and he sank into obscurity and penury – and all because, France would have us believe, the judge who tried the offence charged against Crainquebille was temperamentally conditioned invariably to accept police evidence – the evidence in the tale of Constable 64, otherwise Bastien Matra from Cinto-Monte in Corsica. The salient passage in Mr Justice Hanna's charge ran as follows:

> It does not matter whether a witness is a police-officer or a clergyman, or occupies any other official position; you have to weigh the evidence of every witness with equal care and determine whether you can accept it as trustworthy. Guards are not more sacrosanct than any other class of witness. A great French writer, Anatole France, in his story 'Crainquebille' indicated that judges were too prone to give undue weight to the evidence of official witnesses when they appeared in uniform, and that if the gendarme appeared merely as Jacques Crabot of Corsica, his evidence would not outweigh that of any other civilian. You have to apply the same tests to the evidence of a Guard as to that of any other witness. He is entitled to no more credibility than anyone else with a clear character.

30 Anatole France, *Crainquebille, Putois, Riquet and other profitable tales*, trans. Winifred Stephens (London, 1916). 31 *ILT & SJ*, lxv (1931), 278.

OSCAR WILDE
1854–1900

One Stephen Davis was convicted of murder in 1997. Among the grounds of appeal raised before the Court of Criminal Appeal in Dublin was the contention that the trial judge should have discharged the jury after a number of photographs showing the accused heavily chained had been published in different newspapers. The Court of Criminal Appeal was to dismiss Davis's appeal[32] but, speaking for the court, Mr Justice Hardiman was to deal in general terms with the appearance of prejudicial material in the media. 'The public depiction', the judge observed,[33]

> of any person, but particularly an unconvicted prisoner, wearing the double restraints which are now commonly used in the prison service, is a depiction of him in a position of humiliation and indignity. This is a matter of common experience and has been chronicled by many who have been so depicted or exposed.

Mr Justice Hardiman continued:[34]

> No-one who has read of Oscar Wilde's description of being made to stand in chains on a railway station platform during a transfer from one prison to another can doubt this.

The passage Mr Justice Hardiman alluded to is from *De profundis*:[35]

> Everything about my tragedy has been hideous, mean, repellent, lacking in style; our very dress makes us grotesque. We are the zanies of sorrow. We are clowns whose hearts are broken. We are specially designed to appeal to the sense of humour. On November 13th, 1895, I was brought down here [to Reading Gaol] from London. From two o'clock till half-past two on that day I had to stand on the centre platform of Clapham Junction in convict dress, and handcuffed, for the world to look at. I had been taken out of the hospital ward without a moment's notice being given to me. Of all possible objects I was the most grotesque. When people saw me they laughed. Each train as it came up swelled the audience. Nothing could

32 *The People (D.P.P.) v. Davis* [2001] 1 IR 146. 33 [2001] 1 IR at 150. 34 Ibid. 35 *De profundis* (London, 1911), pp 130–1.

exceed their amusement. That was, of course, before they knew who I was. As soon as they had been informed they laughed still more.

GEORGE BERNARD SHAW
1856–1950

In his will of June 1950 George Bernard Shaw directed his trustee to hold his residuary trust funds on trusts for purposes concerned with the alteration of the English alphabet – a trust for inquiries into the practicability and effect of substituting the proposed new alphabet for the present alphabet of 26 letters, and a trust for transliterating literary work into the proposed new alphabet and publishing it page by page with lettering of the present alphabet opposite. Shaw had specifically in mind the text of his own play 'Androcles and the lion'. Anticipating a possible legal rebuff to his plans, Shaw stipulated that in that event his estate, subject to various legacies and annuities, should be divided equally between the British Museum, the National Gallery of Ireland and the Royal Academy of Dramatic Art.

Shaw's own premonitions were well founded, for in the English Chancery Division in 1957 Mr Justice Harman held that Shaw's trusts in regard to reform of the alphabet were not charitable and that they therefore failed.[36] His wife's will which contained rather different but equally unusual objects, it may be recalled, passed muster: see above, p. 122, under CHARLES DICKENS.

Mr Justice Harman entered into the spirit of the occasion in an evocative opening paragraph in his judgment. 'All his long life', he wrote,[37]

> Bernard Shaw was an indefatigable reformer. He was already well known when the present century dawned, as novelist, critic, pamphleteer, playwright, and during the ensuing half-century he continued to act as a kind of itching powder to the British public, to the English-speaking peoples, and, indeed to an even wider audience, castigating their follies, their foibles and their fallacies, and bombarding them with a combination of paradox and wit that earned him in the course of years the status of an oracle: the Shavian oracle; and the rare distinction of adding a word to the language. Many of his projects he lived to see gain acceptance and carried into effect and become normal. It was natural that he should be interested in English orthography and pronunciation. These are obvious targets for the reformer.

36 *In re Shaw, deceased* [1957] 1 WLR 729. 37 [1957] 1 WLR at 731.

> It is as difficult for the native to defend the one as it is for the foreigner to compass the other. The evidence shows that Shaw had for many years been interested in the subject. Perhaps his best known excursion in this field is 'Pygmalion', in which the protagonist is a professor of phonetics: this was produced as a play in 1914 and has held the stage ever since and invaded the world of the film. It is indeed a curious reflection that this same work, tagged with versicles which I suppose Shaw would have detested and tricked out with music which he would have eschewed (see the preface to the 'Admirable Bashville'), is now charming huge audiences on the other side of the Atlantic and has given birth to the present proceedings. I am told that the receipts from this source have enabled the executors to get on terms with the existing death duties payable on the estate, thus bringing the interpretation of the will into the realm of practical politics.

The residuary legatees, who had successfully objected to Shaw's plans for a 40-letter alphabet, were apparently to agree to set aside a small sum – £8,300 – for a competition for a new alphabet in which in 1962 an edition of *Androcles and the lion* was eventually to be printed.[38]

KENNETH GRAHAME
1859–1932

In *Brady v. Irish National Insurance Co.* in 1986,[39] the scope of standard cover in an insurance policy for a motor cruiser was the subject of analysis by the Irish Supreme Court. Two boats, one of them the plaintiff's motor cruiser, were laid up for the winter at an inland waterway mooring. When working on his boat, the plaintiff partially disconnected the cooking apparatus in the galley, but this was unknown to the owner of the other boat who felt free, when working on his vessel, to avail of the cooking apparatus on his friend's motor cruiser. When seeking to do so, an explosion occurred which caused both personal injury and damage to the plaintiff's motor cruiser. The plaintiff sought an indemnity from his insurer in respect of possible personal injury claims and the damage to the motor cruiser. The insurer demurred, arguing, first, that loss had resulted from the plaintiff's want of due diligence, and, secondly, that there had been a breach of warranty that the cruiser, when laid up, would not be used for any purpose other then 'customary overhauling'. Mr Justice O'Hanlon, held in favour of the insurer, but the Supreme Court, by a 4–1 majority, reversed. An expansive notion

38 *Oxford DNB*, vol. 50, p. 96: entry on Shaw by Stanley Weintraub. 39 [1986] IR 698.

of what was involved in 'overhauling' enabled the court to reach that conclusion.[40] Mr Justice McCarthy, in a concurring judgment, added a flourish of his own:[41]

> The healthy recreation pictured by Kenneth Grahame, *The wind in the willows* (ch. 1) – 'There is *nothing* – absolutely nothing – half so much worth doing as simply messing about in boats',[42] does not negative the ordinary insurance policy applied to pleasure craft.

*

There was to be a further reference to *The wind in the willows* by the Irish Supreme Court in 1998. The *Von Rocks* was a dredger employed to deepen the waters in harbours, channels and estuaries. But was it a 'ship' for purposes of the International Convention on the Arrest of Sea Going Ships, 1952, incorporated into Irish law by the Jurisdiction of Courts (Maritime Convention) Act, 1989? Mr Justice Barr thought not, and thus ordered the *Von Rocks*'s release after its arrest by the Admiralty marshal on foot of on ex parte application. The Supreme Court disagreed, whilst accepting that the dredger lacked several of the characteristics normally associated with a ship. For instance, it was not self-propelled, was not normally manned by a crew and had no steering mechanism.[43]

In an English case decided in 1992,[44] it had been held by Mr Justice Sheen that a jet ski was not a ship within the meaning of the Merchant Shipping Acts. The circumstance that the purpose of a 'jet ski' was 'not to go from one place to another' weighed with the judge. Plainly, however, an approach of that sort to the solution of the definitional problem equally posed by a marine dredger created difficulties, difficulties to which Mr Justice Keane immediately addressed himself in the appeal in the *Van Rocks* case. 'It is questionable, with respect', Mr Justice Keane observed,[45]

> whether to come within the category of a 'ship' the purpose of a craft must be 'to go from one place to another'. In the case of non-commercial craft, it seems somewhat unreal to regard their purpose as being a journey from one point to a specific destination. Yachts which take part in the America's Cup are designed and constructed with a view to testing the excellence of

40 Cf. the judgment of Chief Justice Finlay: [1986] IR at 715. 41 [1986] IR at 721. 42 Water Rat to Mole, *The wind in the willows*, ch. 1: 'The river bank'. 43 *In re the 'Von Rocks'* [1998] 3 IR 41, [1998] 1 ILRM 481. 44 *Steedman v. Scofield* [1992] 2 Lloyd's Rep. 163. 45 [1998] 3 IR at 54–5, [1998] 1 ILRM at 492–3.

> their technology and the seamanship of their crews rather than transporting people from one place to another.

And there was another consideration besides. 'On a less exalted level', Mr Justice Keane noted, in bringing this critical paragraph in his argument to a conclusion,[46]

> people will for long continue to derive enjoyment from being on the sea, not because they are accomplishing a journey to an intended destination but simply for the pleasure of, in the well worn phrase from *The wind in the willows*, 'messing about in boats'.

SIR JAMES MATTHEW BARRIE
1860–1937

It is frequently the case that it is not easy to describe in anything approaching clear and comprehensible language the net issue in a dispute between a taxpayer and the Revenue over the liability to tax of the former. The *St Aubyn* dispute, with its quotation from Homer and set out above, is a case in point.[47] The liability to income tax of Mrs Elsie Bambridge, the daughter of the writer Rudyard Kipling, a question that was argued before Mr Justice Harman in the Chancery Division in 1954, furnishes a second example.[48] Mrs Bambridge inherited investments in Canada from her father under a settlement Kipling had made in 1934, and from her mother, not under her mother's separate settlement which had been revoked, but rather under the latter's will. The ultimate decision of Mr Justice Harman was to hold Mrs Bambridge liable to income tax solely in respect of the investments inherited via her father.

So far as the investments inherited via her father were concerned, Mrs Bambridge argued that ' the associated operations' which, under the relevant clause of the applicable Finance Act,[49] precipitated any liability to income tax, included not just the original settlement and subsequent transfer but also the deaths in succession of the father and mother. These two deaths, it was maintained, could not be regarded as 'associated operations'. Whether to view death in such macabre terms or otherwise was the conundrum that faced Mr Justice Harman. An allusion to words of Peter Pan enabled him to discharge the task

46 [1998] 3 IR at 55, [1998] 1 ILRM at 493. 47 Above, p. 29. 48 *Bambridge v. Inland Revenue Commisioners* [1954] 1 WLR 1265. 49 Finance Act 1936 (26 Geo. V & 1 Edw. VIII, c. 38), s. 18.

before him with a facility that others might choose to envy. 'Death', avers Peter Pan, the judge was to observe,[50] 'is an awfully big adventure, but the Inland Revenue has not yet claimed it is not an associated operation'.

Peter Pan's take on death comes at the end of act 3 of Barrie's drama. This is the scene set in the mermaids' lagoon where Wendy, the lost boys and himself do battle with Hook and the pirates.[51] The climax of the action sees Peter alone on the rock as the waters rise, Peter knowing that it will soon be submerged and himself as well. Though the 'awfully big adventure'[52] was rightly anticipated, relief quite unexpectedly arrives. A nest floats by, Peter arranges a makeshift sail out of his shirt, and escapes – to live another day.

EDMOND ROSTAND
1868–1918

In the Harris Tweed case that wound its way up from the Scottish courts in 1938 to the House of Lords the following year,[53] important clarification of the scope of the tort of conspiracy was the outcome. Union officials representative of dockers and also of mill workers on the island of Lewis in the Outer Hebrides instructed the dockers at Stornoway to refuse to handle yarn imported from the mainland and destined for turning into tweed cloth by the Crofter Hand Woven Harris Tweed Co. and others. Yarn was also produced on the island for processing by a different group of mill-owners, but this yarn was more expensive than yarn imported from the mainland. Hence the union-supported embargo.

Affirming the decision of the Court of Session, the House of Lords held that the predominant purpose of the combination proved to have existed in the case (involving the union officials and, it was apparently accepted, that other group of mill-owners) was the legitimate promotion of the interests of the persons combining and, since the means employed to effect the embargo were neither criminal nor tortious in themselves, the combination itself was not unlawful.

In the course of the leading opinion given in the case, Viscount Simon, the lord chancellor, paused to consider the argument, frequently portrayed in accepted doctrine, that damage inflicted by two persons in unison was more likely to have legal consequences than damage inflicted by a single individual.[54]

50 [1954] 1 WLR at 1268. 51 J.M. Barrie, *Peter Pan and other plays*, ed. with intro by Peter Hollindale (Oxford, 1995), pp 118–25. 52 *Peter Pan*, act 3, line 180. 53 *Crofter Hand Woven Harris Tweed Co. v. Veitch* [1942] AC 435, affirming the Second Division of the Court of Session, 1940 SC 141. 54 [1942] AC at 443–4.

One explanation for such a state of affairs was dismissed by Viscount Simon. 'The view', he declared,[55]

> that the explanation is to be found in the increasing power of numbers to do damage beyond what one individual can do is open to the obvious answer that this depends on the personality and influence of the individual.

An historical analogy is introduced:[56]

> The action of a single tyrant may be more potent to inflict suffering on the continent of Europe than a combination of less powerful persons.

A proposition that could well have featured in an Oxbridge entrance examination, where it would have tested the mettle of Alan Bennett's 'history boys', is, in the law report, preceded by a second analogy – a curious choice this – drawn from French theatre. In the play, Viscount Simon was also to remark,[57]

> Cyrano de Bergerac's single voice was more effective to drive the bad actor Montfleury off the stage than the protests of all the rest of the audience to restrain him.[58]

Asked to explain his antipathy towards Montfleury, Cyrano offers two reasons, each of which, in his estimation, was justification enough. The first of these, unlike the second (which remains a secret) is given in a little detail:[59]

> C'est un acteur déplorable qui gueule,
> Et qui soulève, avec des han! de porteur d'eau,
> Le vers qu'il faut laisser s'envoler!
>
> (An actor villainous! who mouths,
> And heaves up like a bucket from a well
> The verses that should, bird-like, fly!)

Rostand's masterpiece was first performed in Paris in 1897. Montfleury was the stage name of the actor Zacharie Jacob (d. 1667), who is said to have died as a result of his histrionics in the part of Oreste in Jean Racine's *Andromaque*.[60]

55 [1942] AC at 443. 56 Ibid. 57 Ibid. 58 Edmond Rostand, *Cyrano de Bergerac*, act 1, scene 4. 59 Ibid., lines 244–6 (trans.: Project Gutenberg's Etext at www.gutenberg.org/dirs/etext98/cdben10.txt. 60 Rostand, *Cyrano de Bergerac*, ed. Geoff Woollen (London, 1994), p. 227.

The real-life Cyrano de Bergerac (1619–55) abandoned a military career to become a remarkable writer, his authorship embracing plays, essays and satire. Indulging a fertile imagination, Cyrano's satirical oeuvre is claimed to have influenced Molière (*Les fourberies de Scapin*), Voltaire (*Micromégas*), and in the English-speaking world, Jonathan Swift (*Gulliver's travels*).[61]

ROSE MACAULAY
1881–1958

In 1960 the Court of Appeal overturned an award of £7,500 damages in favour of a 6-year-old girl, Dorothy Aldrich, who had fallen through a glass skylight and been severely injured while playing on premises in Paddington, in London, being demolished at the time by the defendants in the case.[62] The accident occurred whilst Dorothy was climbing around in the garage of an empty house. Lord Justice Hodson, in his judgment, accepted the evidence that had been presented which showed that the demolition firm had made frequent efforts to keep children off the site. Children had regularly played there and had become a perfect nuisance. Workmen would chase them away; if the police came along, the children would sing rude songs. Moreover, the children would get hold of workmen's tools, break open stores, place tools on the fire and break down bricks from stacks. Playgrounds may have been few in this particular part of London, but he refused to treat the house or the skylight as an allurement, with all the legal consequences that would then ensue: 'Temptation did not amount to allurement.'[63]

In a concurring judgment, Lord Justice Harman proved equally unsympathetic. An empty house was 'no more an allurement than any other of the thousands of unoccupied houses in London'. He continued:[64]

> No doubt a bombed site had an attraction for children, as had been shown in Miss Rose Macaulay's novel, *The world my wilderness*,[65] the action of which took place entirely on bombed sites. But this particular garage was not the bombed part of this site.

61 *Dictionnaire de biographie française*, ix (Paris, 1961), cols. 145–53 (L. Martal). 62 *Aldrich v. Henry Boyer Ltd.*, *The Times*, 16 Jan. 1960. 63 Ibid. 64 Ibid. 65 First published, 1950. Dame Rose Macaulay's *Pleasure of ruins* (not perhaps totally inapposite either) was published in 1953.

BRYAN MacMAHON
1909–1998

In key decisions, handed down in Dublin in 1995, first the High Court and then, by a majority, the Supreme Court held that it was lawful to withdraw medical treatment from a woman who for over two decades, whilst not in a persistent vegetative state, had only minimal cognitive capacity.[66]

Joining the majority, Mr Justice O'Flaherty ruminates briefly on death – the certain outcome the woman was to face as a consequence of the Supreme Court's decision. In the context, a literary quotation was perhaps far from being dubbed inapposite:[67]

> I move to the concept of death. For those of religious belief, death is not an end but a beginning. In the submissions at bar on behalf of the committee of the ward death was said to be part of life – indeed the only certainty in life. Although, as Bryan MacMahon has written 'each person attempts to mute or cancel the terror of impending death' ('The Storyman' by Bryan MacMahon (1994); Dublin, Poolbeg) in everyone's subconscious there is a hope of a peaceful and dignified death. We console the bereaved when a death occurs unexpectedly if the deceased was spared suffering.

And the judge continued:[68]

> In my judgment, this case is not about terminating a life but only to allow nature to take its course which would have happened even a short number of years ago and still does in places where medical technology has not advanced as far as it has in this country, for example.

66 *In re a Ward of Court (withholding medical treatment) (No. 2)* [1996] 2 IR 79. 67 [1996] 2 IR at 131. 68 Ibid.

An Afterword

There doubtless persist observers who view the phenomenon of literary allusions in court judgments as sheer affectation, an indulgence most assuredly to be disavowed. However this may be, the fact remains that the practice itself is very much alive. Three recent instances of resort to it are recorded in speeches of members of the House of Lords, and if within that august tribunal the value of the practice continues to enjoy acceptance it would appear churlish to argue that the practice itself should be shelved.

In re Deep Vein Thrombosis and Air Travel Group Litigation[1] was a group action first brought before the courts in 2002 to hold a number of international air carriers answerable under the Warsaw Convention of 1929 as amended, and scheduled to the Carriage by Air Act 1961,[2] alleging injury and, in some instances, death following the onset of deep vein thrombosis. To succeed, the group had to show that the onset of this kind of thrombosis could be categorised as an 'accident'. Mr Justice Nelson in 2002, the Court of Appeal (Lord Phillips of Worth Matravers, Lords Justices Judge and Kay) in 2003, and the House of Lords (Lords Scott of Foscote, Steyn, Walker of Gestingthorpe, Baroness Hale of Richmond and Lord Mance) in 2005, in succession, all held that the claim failed. A common thread running through all the judgments handed down was that an 'accident' for purposes of the Warsaw Convention had to be something happening external to the traveller. The onset of deep vein thrombosis did not fit into that category.

One precedent caused a little difficulty – the case of *Husain v. Olympic Airways,* decided by the United States Supreme Court in 2004.[3] Here an asthma sufferer, to whom cigarette smoke represented a health risk, secured a seat in the non-smoking part of the aircraft. On discovering even so that he was only three rows away from the smoking section, he or his wife sought an alternative seat. This could have been arranged but the flight attendant refused to oblige. Murphy's Law now operated. During the flight the asthma sufferer became affected by the ambient smoke from the smoking section and suffered a serious asthma attack from which he died. The Supreme Court held, by a majority, that the widow could succeed in her claim. An Australian judge, Mr Justice Kirby, as

1 [2006] 1 AC 495. 2 9 & 10 Eliz. II, c. 27. 3 (2004) 540 US 644.

Lord Walker of Gestingthorpe was to explain in the House of Lords case, had shown that in *Husain* there were, as that judge phrased it,[4]

> peculiar features of the confrontation between the wife, the passenger and the flight attendant ... that arguably lifted that case from classification as a 'non-event' [nothing external to the passenger] into classification as an unexpected happening or event and hence an 'accident'.

Lord Walker concluded his judgment with an analogy drawn from crime fiction (not that that analogy, with the benefit of hindsight, might be adjudged by some the most apposite). 'The same approach', he argued,[5]

> can be found in a very familiar literary source. In Conan Doyle's *Silver Blaze* Sherlock Holmes draws Dr Watson's attention 'To the curious incident of the dog in the night-time'. 'That was the curious incident': cited in the *Oxford Dictionary of Quotations*, 4th ed. (rev.) (1996), p. 256, para. 14. The dog's failure to bark was part of a more complex incident in which an intruder came into the stable yard in the middle of the night, and was evidently not a stranger to the dog.[6]

Silver Blaze was a racehorse, the favourite to win the Wessex Cup. When both the horse and its trainer, the retired jockey John Straker, mysteriously disappeared shortly before the scheduled race, Sherlock Holmes was summoned by telegram by Silver Blaze's owner, Colonel Ross, to assist with the investigation. Holmes's sleuthing resulted in the local constabulary's prime suspect, Fitzroy Simpson, being declared innocent and the unveiling of a betting scam involving Straker who had in the meantime been found dead. Straker's plan had been to remove Silver Blaze from its stable in the middle of the night, unannounced and unobserved, and then lame the horse. Three stable lads on guard duty posed a problem. Ned Hunter, the boy who slept in the stable, was taken care of by being given a meal of drugged curried mutton. The two other boys sleeping in the chaff-cutting loft above the harness room in the stable were to pass the night of the critical kidnapping quite undisturbed. Silver Blaze made no fuss over being removed from the stable by Straker who had been immediately recognised. In consequence, the dog did not bark – Holmes's 'curious incident', recalled by Lord Walker. And it was to be Silver Blaze who was the author of Straker's own destruction when Straker produced the knife to lame him.[7]

4 See *Povey v. Qantas Airways Ltd* (2005) 223 CLR 189 at 245–6. 5 [2006] 1 AC at 511. 6 Holmes's exchange was with Inspector Gregory of the local constabulary, not Watson. 7 For the full story see Sir Arthur Conan Doyle, *The Penguin complete adventures of Sherlock Holmes* (London, 1984), p. 335.

A challenge presented by what was regarded as unguarded language by a member of the Court of Appeal had led a law lord in 2003, in joining his colleagues in allowing an appeal, to issue a strong rebuff. In an extraordinary turn of events, what we witness is a reprise by Lord Hoffmann of one of the more celebrated episodes recorded in Homer's *Odyssey.*[8]

On a warm Bank Holiday weekend in 1995 an 18-year-old youth visiting Brereton Heath Park in Cheshire decided to go in for a swim in the lake in the park, formerly a disused quarry. Swimming, however, was prohibited as notices on display indicated and as park rangers were wont to inform visitors. Again, Murphy's Law operated. Standing in shallow water, John Tomlinson executed a dive. His head struck the sandy bottom, the injuries were considerable and he became a tetraplegic, paralysed from the neck down. Mr Justice Jack held that the risk of injury from diving in the way Mr Tomlinson had executed it was obvious and that the two local authorities sued were not answerable. By a majority, the Court of Appeal (Lords Justices Ward and Sedley; Lord Justice Longmore dissenting) disagreed. Lord Justice Ward highlighted the gravity of the risk, the failure of the warning notices to curtail the extent to which that risk was run, and the continuing attraction to would-be swimmers of the beach and lake. A little later in his judgment Lord Justice Ward added a sentence, which expanded on this last consideration. 'The authorities', he reasoned, 'were inviting public use of the amenity knowing that the water was a siren call strong enough to turn stout men's minds'.[9]

The House of Lords unanimously overturned the decision of the Court of Appeal majority. Among the several speeches, that of Lord Hobhouse of Woodborough is remarkable for its attack on the notion that obvious dangers in the open air had to be the object of preventive measures and warning notices. 'Does', he asks,[10]

> the law require that all trees be cut down because some youths may climb them and fall? Does the law require the coastline and other beauty spots to be lined with warning notices?

But it is the passage in the speech of Lord Hoffmann which merits special mention here. He took immediate exception to Lord Justice Ward's identification of the water at the Brereton Heath Park as constituting 'a siren call'. 'This',

8 Book 12. 9 *Tomlinson v. Congleton Borough Council* [2004] 1 AC 46. 10 [2004] 1 AC at 96–97.

together with Tomlinson's counsel's argument that the defendants had been 'luring people into a deathtrap', he judged 'gross hyperbole'.[11] He went on:[12]

> The trouble with the island of the Sirens was not the state of the premises. It was that the Sirens held mariners spellbound until they died of hunger. The beach, give or take a fringe of human bones,[13] was an ordinary Mediterranean beach. If Odysseus had gone ashore and accidentally drowned himself having a swim, Penelope would have had no action against the Sirens for luring him there with their songs. Likewise in this case, the water was perfectly safe for all normal activities ... It is a mere circularity to say that a failure to stop people getting into the water was an omission which gave rise to a duty to take steps to stop people from getting into the water.

It is Lord Hoffmann again who was responsible for another literary foray in *Oxfordshire Co. Council v. Oxford City Council*, decided in 2006.[14] This case was concerned with identifying for the benefit of the county council, the appropriate registration authority, the exact consequences to flow from the registration of a patch of land as a town or village green under the salient legislation as amended.[15] The land on the fringes of Oxford itself was known as the Trap Grounds, and it was on this land that the city council wished to build houses. The applicant for registration had somewhat different ideas. A track leading from the Trap Grounds and known as Frog Lane had some interesting literary as well as historical associations, as Lord Hoffmann was to recall. 'The Trap Grounds', he reported,[16]

> no doubt looked very different before they were cut off, first by the 18th century canal and then by the 19th century railway, from the great north Oxford common of Port Meadow. In those days Frog Lane was called My Lady's Way and led across the Meadow to the nunnery at Godstow where Charles Dodgson and Alice Liddell picnicked and fair Rosamund, mistress of Henry II, lies buried.

11 [2004] 1 AC at 80. 12 Ibid. 13 Circe explained to Odysseus about the bones: πολύς δ'ἀμφ' ὀστεόφιν θὶς ἀνδρῶν πυθομένων, περὶ δὲ ῥινοὶ μινύθουσι: about them [the Sirens seated in a meadow] is a great heap of bones of mouldering men, and round the bones the skin is wasting. *Odyssey*, xii, lines 45–6. 14 [2006] 2 AC 674. 15 Commons Registration Act 1965 (1965, c.64), as amended by Countryside and Rights of Way Act 2000 (2000, c.37). 16 [2006] 2 AC at 684.

An initial difficulty that arose regarding the Trap Grounds was, as a report commissioned by the county council had occasion to point out, the fact that about one third of the surface was permanently under water and the rest was scrubland, in relation to which only 25 per cent was 'reasonably accessible to the hardy walker'.[17] The description accorded the grounds by Lord Walker of Gestingthorpe was somewhat blunter:[18] it was 'an overgrown, rubble-strewn, semi-submerged area'. The Trap Grounds were thus scarcely idyllic and, as members of the House of Lords did not fail to point out, were certainly at odds with the image of the traditional village green.

That image, Lord Hoffmann averred, was 'a creation of the literature of sensibility in the late 18th century'[19] – an assertion he sought to support with a quotation from Oliver Goldsmith's poem, 'The deserted village',[20] where perhaps the best mental picture in literature of a village green had been depicted. The green at Auburn – the village inspired by Lissoy, Co. Westmeath – was a place, Lord Hoffmann reminded us, where

> … toil, remitting, lent its turn to play,
> And all the village train, from labour free,
> Led up their sports beneath the spreading tree!
> While many a pastime circled in the shade,
> The young contending as the old survey'd;
> And many a gambol frolick'd o'er the ground,
> And sleights of art and feats of strength went round;
> And still, as each repeated pleasure tired,
> Succeeding sports the mirthful band inspired …

The Trap Grounds were very different. But that did not mean they were to be denied entry into the critical legal category of a village green. As Lord Hoffmann himself asserted:[21]

> No doubt there were, and perhaps are village greens like that [at Auburn] but the law took a more prosaic view of the matter. It was not particularly concerned with the spreading tree and the ancient turf but simply with whether there was an immemorial custom for inhabitants of a parish borough or similar locality to use the land for sports and pastimes.

17 Quoted by Lord Hoffmann: [2006] 2 AC at 683–84. 18 [2006] 2 AC at 721. 19 [2006] 2 AC at 684. 20 There is a fine illustrated edition of the poem brought out by the Gallery Press, Loughcrew, Oldcastle, Co. Meath: Oliver Goldsmith, *The deserted village*, intro. Vera Groarke, illustr. Blaise Drummond (Oldcastle, Co. Meath, 2002). 21 [2006] 2 AC at 684–85.

It is worth remarking that Baroness Hale of Richmond in her judgment in the same case approached the identification of the pertinent rural idyll in a rather different fashion. Town and village greens, she wrote,[22] are

> not just picturesque reminders of a by-gone age. They are a very present amenity to the communities they serve. The village green in Scorton, in the North Riding of Yorkshire, is a perfect example.

Nor has the practice of quoting from literary sources been disowned in another senior Commonwealth tribunal – the High Court of Australia. Here a not unattractive citation from the book of Psalms is recorded in 1998. The context was supplied by an accident that had occurred seven years earlier.

On 16 February 1991 a Mr Johnson was camping with others on the Blackwood River in the south-west of Western Australia at a place called Sue's Bridge Crossing. A length of rope was attached to a branch of a tree alongside the river. Mr Johnson took hold of it and swung out over the river. Unfortunately, the rope gave way and Mr Johnson fell to the river bank. In the process he suffered severe injury to his right foot.

Mr Johnson lodged a claim under an individual injury and sickness policy. This covered injury 'resulting in ... permanent total loss of use of one limb'. 'Limb' was defined to include 'a foot at or above the ankle'. The facts as found showed that Mr Johnson was severely restricted in the use to which he was able to put his foot. Successive courts in Western Australia held that Mr Johnson had not proved that he had suffered permanent total loss of his foot within the meaning of the insurance policy. The High Court of Australia by a majority (Chief Justice Brennan, Mr Justice McHugh, Mr Justice Gummow, Mr Justice Hayne; Mr Justice Kirby dissenting) dismissed a further appeal: *Johnson v. American Home Assurance.*[23] The lone dissentient, Mr Justice Kirby, who unavailingly was to spearhead a novel approach to the interpretation of the critical clause in Mr Johnson's insurance contract, commenced his judgment with a pleasing biblical flourish:[24]

> The ninety-first Psalm reflects the common human fear of injury to the foot. The Psalmist promises rescue from various misfortunes. The angels, we are assured, will take charge over the righteous:

22 [2006] 2 AC at 721. 23 (1998) 192 CLR 266. 24 192 CLR at 268.

> They shall bear thee up in their hands, lest thou dash thy foot against a stone.

> Unfortunately, angels did not intervene to protect the appellant's foot.[25] But he had an insurance policy. This case concerns his attempt to obtain earthly rescue from the insurer. The question is whether the courts below misconstrued the policy.

Mr Justice Kirby more recently mounted another literary foray. This was in the Australian case of *Povey* v. *Qantas Airways Ltd.*,[26] where it was also sought to have the onset of deep vein thrombosis during an air flight adjudged an accident. Mr Justice Kirby commenced his judgment with a spirited paragraph replete with a number of classical and other allusions:[27]

> Since ancient times, human beings have known of the dangers of flight. The mythologies of Greece, Crete, Persia and other lands include stories of injurious attempts by men and women to soar into the firmament ... In his *Metamorphoses* [Book VIII, lines 183–235] Ovid describes the winged flight of Daedalus and Icarus, brought to an end by the youth's reckless attempt to soar too high.

Here it is only right to furnish the Latin and an English version of lines 225–26 of book VIII:

> rapidi vicinia solis mollit odoratas, pennarum vincula, ceras.

> (the searching rays of the sun had softened the fragrant wax which held together Icarus's wings.)

Mr Justice Kirby continued, after this allusion,[28]

> The appellant in this case [Mr Povey] ... complains of an injury [the onset of the thrombosis] caused by his air travel [from Sydney to London and return]. However, whereas Icarus had only his father Daedalus to assist him in his peril, the appellant has the Warsaw Convention. To that Convention he has appealed. But, as I shall explain, it is to no greater avail.

25 Psalm 91, v. 12. 26 (2005) 223 CLR 189. 27 223 CLR at 219. 28 Ibid.; Ovid, *Metamorphoses*, bks. I–VIII, trans. F.J. Miller (Loeb Classical Lib., Cambridge, MA and London, 1960), pp 422–3.

The outcome thus anticipated that reached by the House of Lords in *In re Deep Vein Thrombosis and Air Travel Group Litigation*.[29]

Literary quotation and allusion discoverable in the judgments of the courts almost always have their authorship identified by the judge responsible for bringing them into service. In a few instances for this book some sleuthing was required where the judge omitted to do anything of the sort. So it turned out in the cases of Hesiod and Martial alluded to in judgments penned at a time when a classical education was de rigueur, something very obviously which it is not today.

Despite an amount of sleuthing, and the summoning of assistance from professors of English, whose identity I prefer to keep secret but whose efforts on my behalf I most gratefully acknowledge, there exist in the law reports two judgments littered with literary quotation, the sources for which I was not able to track down.

Somewhat curiously, these judgments represent the intellectual effort of the same man, John David Fitzgerald, who as Lord Fitzgerald was the first Irish lawyer to be appointed a law lord, a post he held from 1882 until his death in 1889. A pleasing cameo of Fitzgerald was penned by another Irish law lord, Lord Lowry, in 2001.[30] Of Fitzgerald's judgments in the House of Lords, Lowry was to write that they

> were undemonstrative but ... notable for their clarity and their relevance to the main point in the case. Their author also had the happy knack of being right. His deep learning ranged widely and his statutory interpretation is impossible to fault. In short, he was a very good judge.

The two cases with the as yet unidentified literary quotations both hail from the 1880s. There is another similarity. Both, as it happens, are Scottish appeals: *Thomson v. Weems* (1884) and *Caird v. Sime* (1887). I shall deal with them in that order.

A Scot, one William Weems, and later to be elected provost of the town of Johnstone, took out a life assurance policy. The proposal form had asked Weems to answer this question: was he temperate? And had he always been so? The replies Weems supplied were later held to be at total variance with the true state of things – Weems having been adjudged to be an inveterate toper – so much so

29 [2006] 1 AC 495. 30 Lord Lowry, 'The Irish lords of appeal in ordinary', in D.S. Greer and N.M. Dawson (ed.), *Mysteries and solutions in Irish legal history* (Dublin, 2001), p. 193 at pp 193–5.

indeed that the House of Lords, overruling the Second Division of the Court of Session, held that the life assurance policy in question was null and void.[31]

Literary figures (unidentified) were to receive an outing in the speech of Lord Fitzgerald. "'Temperance in habits'", he argued,[32]

> is a sentence to be interpreted, and though not to be taken in the Pythagorean sense of 'total abstinence', yet seems to import abstemiousness, or at least moderation –
>
> 'The rule of "not too much,"
> By temperance taught'.

There was more to come. 'The evidence for the defenders', Lord Fitzgerald resumed,[33]

> is not in my judgement displaced by the negative evidence led for the pursuers. The cause of death, too, is confirmation strongly of the assured having fallen into that fatal habit which produces
>
> '... all the kinds
> Of maladies that lead to death's grim cave
> Wrought by intemperance.'

It was against this danger that the insurers of course had sought protection.

Three years later, in *Caird v. Sime*, Lord Fitzgerald produced another set of quotations that, so far as the author of this compendium is concerned, continue to defy identification. But first a description of the context for Fitzgerald's remarks.

Professor Caird, Professor of Moral Philosophy at the University of Glasgow, in the 1880s discovered to his consternation that a local bookseller, Sime, was retailing copies of his university lectures in pamphlet form. In 1884 the sheriff-substitute in the Sheriff Court of Lanarkshire agreed that there had been a breach of copyright and granted Caird a perpetual interdict. When Sime appealed to the Court of Session, no less than thirteen judges were consulted. Nine of these accepted that the pamphlets did in fact reproduce the professor's lectures but, as regards the claim based on copyright, the judges were divided, half of those expressing an opinion taking the view that Caird had a right of

31 *Thomson v. Weems* (1884) 9 App. Cas. 671. 32 9 App. Cas. at 697. 33 9 App. Cas. at 698.

property in his lectures, the other half deciding otherwise. The interlocutor drawn up based on these conflicting opinions was somewhat ambiguous but, treating it as a defeat, Caird appealed to the House of Lords where a majority of the three law lords, Lord Halsbury, the lord chancellor, and Lord Watson, upheld the appeal and affirmed the granting of a perpetual interdict or injunction.[34] A delivery of lectures to an undergraduate class at a university was 'not a communication to the public at large'; Professor Caird was thus entitled to restrain others from publishing these lectures without his consent.

The Irish lord of appeal in ordinary, Lord Fitzgerald, dissented. Agreeing with one half of the Scots judges, he held that there had occurred just that communication with the public at large. A comment of the sheriff-substitute in his decision in favour of Caird attracted Fitzgerald's particular ire. The sheriff-substitute sensed it strengthened the professor's claim that his lectures would be unlikely to change from year to year. Fitzgerald attacked the logic, basing his argument on what he perceived to be the proper responsibility of any university lecturer worth his salt.

The sheriff-substitute's contention, Lord Fitzgerald began,[35]

> would seem to assimilate the professor's duty to the cuckoo cry of repetition. I rather think that this eminent professor would repudiate such a suggestion, and tell us that the lecturer should remember that
>
> 'Beneath this starry arch
> Naught resteth or is still',
>
> and that his duty is to watch over and criticize new modes of thought, new works, the march of intellect, and those discoveries which
>
> 'Make old knowledge
> Pale before the new.'

'Even in pure mathematics,' Lord Fitzgerald continued,[36] 'there may be alterations and additions, and ethical science is not free from the inexorable law of mutability.'

34 *Caird v. Sime* (1887) 12 App. Cas. 326. 35 12 App. Cas. at 354. 36 Ibid.

Bibliography

Aesop, *Fables*, trans. and intro. Laura Gibbs (Oxford, 2002)
Aristophanes, *The Frogs*, ed. and trans. Jeffrey Henderson (Cambridge, MA and London, 2002)
Arnold, Matthew, *Poems*, ed. Miriam Allott, 2nd ed. (London and New York, 1979)
Arnott, W.G., 'Swan songs', *Greece and Rome*, 2nd series, xxiv (1977) 149
Avery, Harry C., 'My tongue swore, but my mind unsworn', *Transactions of the American Philosophical Society*, xcix (1968) 19
Avianus, ed. J.W. Duff and A.M. Duff (Cambridge, MA, 1934)
Barrie, J.M., *Peter Pan and other plays*, ed. Peter Hollindale (Oxford, 1995)
Booth, J.B., *London town* (London, 1929)
Boswell, Samuel, *Life of Johnson*, ed. J.W. Cooper (London, 1860)
Bourke, Angela, *The burning of Bridget Cleary* (London, 1999)
Brewer's dictionary of phrase and fable, revised ed. Ivor H. Evans (London, 1975)
Byron, George Gordon, *The complete poetical works*, ed. Jerome J. McCann, 6 vols (Oxford, 1986)
Cicero, *Tusculan disputations*, trans. J.E. King (London and Cambridge, MA, 1966)
Curran, John Adye, KC, *Reminiscences* (London, 1915)
Dickens, Charles, *Our mutual friend* (London, 1865)
——, *A tale of two cities* (London, 1859)
Dictionnaire de biographie française, ix (Paris, 1961)
Doyle, Sir Arthur Conan, *The Penguin complete adventures of Sherlock Holmes* (London, 1984)
Dumas, Alexandre, père, *The count of Monte Cristo* (1846)
Eliot, T.S., *Poems, 1909–1925* (London, 1925)
Fitzgerald, Edward, *Rubáiyát of Omar Khayyám* (1st ed., London, 1859; 4th ed., London, 1879)
France, Anatole, *Crainquebille, Putois, Riquet and other profitable tales*, trans. Winifred Stephens (London, 1916)
France, Peter (ed.), *The new Oxford companion to literature in French* (Oxford, 1995)
Gay, John, *Poetical works*, ed. G.C. Faber (New York, 1926)
Gerald of Wales, *The journey through Wales and The description of Wales*, trans. and intro. Lewis Thorpe (London, 1978)
Gillies, Alexander, *Goethe's Faust: an interpretation* (Oxford, 1957)
Goldsmith, Oliver, *The deserted village*, intro. Vera Groarhe, illustr. Blaise Drummond (Oldcastle, Co. Meath, 2002)
Gordon, Gerald H., *The criminal law of Scotland*, 2nd ed. (Edinburgh, 1978)
Groot, Roger D. 'Isolt's trial and ordeal: a legal-historical analysis' in Paul Brand, Kevin Costello and W.N. Osborough (eds), *Adventures of the law: proceedings of the 16th British Legal History Conference, Dublin 2003* (Dublin, 2005), pp. 1–18
Hesiod, *Works and days*, trans. H.G. Evelyn-White (Cambridge, MA, 1959)
Heuston, R.F.V., '*Liversidge v. Anderson* in retrospect', *Law Quarterly Review*, lxxxvi (1970) 33
Highet, Gilbert, *Juvenal the satirist: a study* (Oxford, 1954)
Homer, *The Iliad done into English verse*, trans. Andrew Lang, Walter Leef and Ernest Myers (London, 1883)
——, *The Odyssey*, bks 1–12, trans. A.T. Murray, revised G.E. Dimock (Cambridge, MA and London, 1995)

Hood, Thomas, *Selected poems*, ed. and intro. John Clubbe (Cambridge, MA, 1970)
Horace, *Satires*, trans. H.R. Fairclough (Cambridge, MA, 1978)
Hoskin, Andrew, *Nothing like a dame: the scandals of Shirley Porter* (London, 2006)
Jefferson, Michael, *Criminal law*, 7th ed. (Harlow, Essex, 2006)
Kilroy, Thomas, *The big chapel* (London, 1971)
Lamb, Charles, *Essays of Elia and Eliana* (London, 1867)
Longford, Elizabeth, *Wellington: pillar of state* (London, 1972)
Lowry, Lord, 'The Irish lords of appeal in ordinary', in D.S. Greer and N.M. Dawson (eds), *Mysteries and solutions in Irish legal history* (Dublin, 2001), pp 193–216
Lucilius, *Satires* (Paris, 1978)
Macauley, Rose, *The pleasure of ruins* (London, 1953)
——, *The world my wilderness* (London, 1950)
MacManus, Francis, *The greatest of these* (Dublin, 1943)
Martial, *Book XIII: The Xenia*, intro. and commentary by T.J. Leary (London, 2001)
Megarry, R.E., *Miscellany-at-law: a diversion for lawyers and others* (London, 1955)
Melville, Herman, *Moby Dick* (New York, 1851)
Milton, John, *The works*, iv (New York, 1931)
New Jerusalem Bible (London, 1985)
Newark, F.H., *Elegantia juris: selected writings*, ed. F.J. McIvor (Belfast, 1973)
O'Connor, Frank (ed.), *A book of Ireland* (London and Glasgow, 1959)
Omar Khayyám, *The Rubáiyát*, ed. A.J. Arberry (London, 1949)
Osborough, W.N., 'Another country, other days: revisiting Thomas Kilroy's *The big chapel*', *Irish University Review*, xxxii (2002) 39
——, 'Executive failure to enforce judicial decrees: a neglected chapter in nineteenth-century constitutional history' in John McEldowney and Paul O'Higgins (eds), *The common law tradition: essays in Irish legal history* (Dublin, 1990), pp 85–116
——, *Studies in Irish legal history* (Dublin, 1999)
Osler, D.G., 'Specificatio in Scots law' in R. Evans-Jones (ed.), *The civil law tradition in Scots law* (Edinburgh, 1995), pp 100–27
Oxford dictionary of national biography, 60 vols (Oxford, 2004)
Ovid, *Metamorphoses*, bks. I–VIII, trans. F.J. Miller (Cambridge, MA and London, 1960)
Perry, Ben, *Aesopica* (Urbana, IL, 1952)
Plato, *Laws*, trans. R.G. Bury, 2 vols (London and Cambridge, MA, 1967–8)
Pliny, *Natural history*, trans. H. Rackham (Cambridge, MA, 1956)
Plunkett, E.A., 'Attorneys and solicitors in Ireland' in *Record of the centenary of the charter of the Incorporated Law Society of Ireland, 1852–1952* (Dublin, 1953), pp 38–74
Pope, Alexander, *The poems*, ed. John Butt (London and New York, 1992)
Richardson, Ruth, *Death, dissection and the destitute* (London, 1987)
Rostand, Edmond, *Cyrano de Bergerac*, ed. Geoff Woollen (London, 1994)
Schama, Simon, *Landscape and memory* (London, 1995)
Simpson, A.W.B., *Cannibalism and the common law* (London, 1986)
Singh, Rabinder, and Thomas, David, 'Human rights implications of a ban on hunting with dogs', *European Human Rights Law Review*, vii (2002) 28
Strabo, *The geography*, trans. H.L. Jones, 8 vols (London and Cambridge, MA, 1960–7)
Strassburg, Gottfried von, *Tristan* (Harmondsworth, Middlesex, 1960)
Suetonius, *De vita Caesarum*, trans. J.C. Rolfe, 2 vols (Cambridge, MA and London, 1979)
Surtees, R.S., *Handley Cross, or the Spa Hunt* (London, 1843)
Tacitus, *The Agricola and the Germania*, trans. H. Mattingly, revised S.A. Handford (London, 1970)
Tennyson, Alfred, *Poems* (London, 1976)

——, *The Works* (London, 1911)

Tennyson, Charles, *Alfred Tennyson* (New York, 1949)

The laws and acts of parliament made by King James the First, … [to] King Charles the Second … collected … by Sir Thomas Murray … (Edinburgh, 1681)

Todd, M.G., *Life of Sophia Jex-Blake* (London, 1918)

Trial of the major war criminals before the International Military Tribunal, Nuernberg, Germany, 14 Nov. 1945–1 Oct. 1946, 42 vols (Nuernberg, 1947–9)

Trollope, Anthony, *The Kellys and the O'Kellys* (London, 1848)

Valerius, Maximus, *Memorable doings and sayings*, ed. and trans. D.R. Shackleton Bailey, 2 vols (Cambridge, MA and London, 2000)

Virgil, *Eclogues and Aeneid I–VI: in English verse*, trans. Charles Bowen (London, 1887)

—, *The Aeneid*, trans. C. Day Lewis (London, 1961)

Wilde, Oscar, *A woman of no importance* (London, 1894)

—, *De profundis* (London, 1911)

Wilson, W.A., *Introductory essays on Scots law* (Edinburgh, 1978)

Zola, Emile, *La curée* (Paris, 1871)

Table of cases

Table of statutes

UNITED KINGDOM

SCOTLAND

IRELAND

IFS/RI

NORTHERN IRELAND

AUSTRALIA (VICTORIA)

USA

Index